A Kept Woman

Lynnette Tiller Appling

Foreword by Tommi Femrite

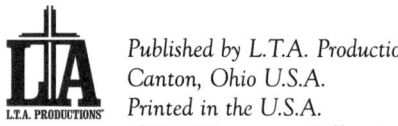

Published by L.T.A. Productions
Canton, Ohio U.S.A.
Printed in the U.S.A.
©2005 Lynnette Tiller Appling. All Rights Reserved.
No part of this book may be reproduced, stored in a retrieval system or transmitted by any means without the written permission of the author.

Formerly published by AuthorHouse 2005
Revised Version published by L.T.A. Productions 2005

ISBN # *0-977489-0-0*

Unless otherwise noted Scripture quotations are from the New King James Version Copyright ©1979, 1980, 1982 by Thomas Nelson, Inc., Used by Permission.
Scripture quotations marked BET are from The Basic English Translation Bible Copyright © 2002 by BibleOcean.com, published and distributed by Valusoft of THO Inc. "The Bible Collection Deluxe". Used by Permission.
Scripture quotations marked ASV are from the American Standard Bible Copyright © 2002 by BibleOcean.com, published and distributed by Valusoft of THO Inc. "The Bible Collection Deluxe". Used by Permission.
Scripture quotations marked AMP are from The Amplified Bible Copyright © 1954, 1958, 1962, 1964, 1965, 1987 by The Lockman Foundation. All Rights Reserved. Used by Permission.

Professional photos of Jeffery and Lynnette Appling, the Appling children and the Appling family are by United Studios of America © 2004

Lyrics of songs and poems that are expressed in this book are the original work of Lynnette Tiller Appling from the CD's entitled From Within Psalms of Lament © 2000, 2001 and Intimate Worship © 2003, 2004 by L.T.A. Productions © 1999, 2000, 2001, 2002, 2003, 2004, 2005. All Rights Reserved.

This is a true story about the life of Lynnette Appling. Names of some individuals and the names of places have been omitted for the protection of the Appling Family and other entities and individuals associated to the events, places and people or the Appling Family.

Book Graphics & Cover by Dawn L. Cobb -Vision Direct
Edited by Tommi Femrite and Carri Bell

Especially for You

To

Name: _____

From

Name: _____

Dedications

This collection of seasons is dedicated to the memories of:

My father **James William Tiller, Sr.**, though our time was brief I will always remember the good days, the smiles, the jokes and the love. Your free spirit is what I valued most. Even until the end you were free. This is what I choose to hold on to. This is the memory I will never forget. I love you Daddy.

My father and grandfather, **Forrest Lowe, Sr.**, when my father dropped out, you stepped in. Now I am married to a man who walks through life just like you. If I never said it before, thank you for teaching me what it means to love. I love you.

My mother and grandmother, **Gretchen Juanita Lowe**, I'll never forget the phone calls you made to me when I was running you kept me on a foundation. In the dark pit that only you knew about, you met me and carried me out. I can't wait to see you again. I love you.

And my son, **Malachi,** it's been a long time, yet I know I will see, hold and kiss you again. With every breath I take, I know you are taking it too. Mommy continuously loves you.

May all of you rest in peace and in the complete knowledge that we will see each other again...soon.

Contents

Foreword

Elder Tommi Femrite	8
A Word From The Author	11
A Kept Woman	12

Epoch 1

Fatherless
Fatherless	17
The Path	19
The Butterfly	24

The Fugitive
Running	29
Bleeding	30
Misplaced Trust	32
The Mistake	33
My Angel	35
Malachi	37
The Death	39
The Funeral	42
Breathing Again	43
Shaila, Joshua and Garra	45

Deep Wounds
    Revelation   53
    Emptiness   56

The Covenant
    Learning To Trust   67
    Finding True Love   70

The Awakening
    The Anointing   81

Epoch 2

My Boaz
    Preparation   88
    Meeting Jeff   90
    Confirmation   92
    Breaking Old Chains   95
    The Wedding Gift   99
    The Wedding Day   100
    The Garden   102

Embryonic
    Treasure Hunting   109
    Seeing His Eyes   109
    From Within: Psalms of Lament   111

The Birthing Process
    Defining The Purpose   117
    L.T.A. Productions   118
    Understanding the True Vision   120
    Ladies Night Out, Inc   122

Quizzes, Test and Exams

Overcoming Hurting People	129
Overcoming The Spirit of Fear	131
Spiritual Chemical Warfare	134
The Ultimate Challenge	137
Intimate Worship	144

Epoch 3

Understanding with Wisdom

Discerning His Heart	153
Little Twiggy	154
Seasonal Acquaintances and Lifetime Friends	156
The Last Mile	159
Giving Up the Call	162
The Power of Spiritual Mothers	164
The Power of Spiritual Sisters	167
Restoration Thru Spiritual Fathers	168
Firmly Planted	169

Epoch 4

Established

The Promise	175
Established	184
A Call For The Broken	186

Foreword

By Tommi Femrite

One of the most difficult God-given assignments we as Christians have is to overcome the pain of our past. Far too often we read autobiographies by Christians who have a powerful testimony but it is left up to us to determine the life lessons and how to apply these lessons personally. *A Kept Woman* is not just a book about Lynnette Appling's testimony, it is a practical mentoring tool filled with nuggets that empowers the reader and gives step-by-step actions to apply to one's life.

There comes a time in each of our lives when we begin to ask why we are here on earth, what our purpose is or even what our call is. God has incredible plan for each of our lives. He has called women to walk in wholeness, authority, victory, dominion, love and much more.

Satan does not know the destiny God has ordained for your life, but he does know God intends to use you to make a difference in the lives of those you come in contact with. Satan writes over the plan of God for your life using the pen of painful situations, abusive circumstances and sorrowful events.

He clearly uses situations and people- even Christians- to wound us. He only needs one situation to occur one time to devastate us. There are multitudes of women who have experienced wounding by Satan. Some have a one time wound and others like Lynnette have been wounded time after time.

This wounding is intended to immobilize us as women forever. The scars that we carry affect the way we view ourselves, others and even God. Unless we allow the healing and restorative power of the Lord to cauterize our wounds, we will continue to walk through this life as weak, depressed, powerless, ineffective victims.

But God has a destiny for you as woman. God writes over the plans of the enemy with the blood of Jesus. The Lord's plan is for you to walk throughout your life strong, full of joy, powerful and victorious! I like God's plan much better...and I have chosen His plan for my life.

Lynnette masterfully weaves her testimony of coming from the place of victim to the place of victorious. As you read, I encourage you to glean from the wisdom of this young woman. You can learn from her mistakes and wrong choices. You can embrace the promises of God and make godly choices. The most important of these choices is to choose to forgive those who have wounded you. Forgiveness sets you free from bondage.

A Kept Woman is a work of beauty and it reflects the Father's heart of how He created you as a woman. Throughout, Lynnette inserts powerful word pictures that bring revelation to the reader. Without preaching, she summarizes her lessons learned and keeps the reader involved while at the same time bringing hope as she tells her story moving from one epoch to the next.

Often people look at a woman in ministry and think they are so incredible because they have never experienced problems or pain like we have. Lynnette puts this wrongful thinking to flight. She openly shares numerous painful events and wrong choices she made that the enemy used to try to silence her, destroy her and even kill her.

But God had a better plan for her life from before the foundations of the earth. The same is true for you. God had a plan for your life even before you were in your mother's womb. Satan has been working overtime to thwart God's plan. Perhaps you have experienced abandonment, fatherlessness, the death of a child, adultery, fornication, rape, physical abuse, emotional abuse, sexual abuse, divorce or being a single parent.

Satan comes to steal, kill and destroy. His job description has not changed. He is out to steal from you, to bring death to you, your relationships and call, to totally destroy you. Lynnette experienced these assaults and even more. Satan continued to torment her after she became a Christian. He moved through other Christians and even leaders in the church. We erroneously think that if we are a Christian, Satan cannot harm us. Perhaps you, like Lynnette, have wondered if there is any hope to be free.

Lynnette melodiously releases the songs of freedom as she writes. She trumpets the sound of hope...Help is on the way! His name is Jesus! He leads with His strong and mighty right arm. But God is no respecter of persons and He will lead you too! He has come to give you life more abundantly. His plans for you are for good and not for evil. He came to restore, repair and renew you. Get ready! Help IS on the way!

Tommi Femrite
Founder & President
Gatekeepers International

A Word From The Author

*If I were to ask you, "What is **A Kept Woman**" you would probably reveal to me that this type of woman is something of disgust. The majority of people would say this is a woman who hunts and uses other women's possessions as her prey. You could never understand this woman for she sells her soul and her body to be kept by a man in luxury.*

Some of you would even secretly wish at times it were you. Surreptitiously in your heart you wish you could just experience the comfort and security this woman must have in knowing she is kept. Either way, she is held as a mistress to some and a marvel to all.

I would personally introduce this woman as one who understands the process of covenant. This type of woman knows who she is and exactly what she is doing. She has the skill to receive what she desires and understands that she can ask what she will and her lover will supply her needs. There is no contract signed, yet there is a promise of being provided for as long as she remains faithful to the man and the situation.

I am here to tell you that God has made a covenant with you since the beginning of time. You, my friend are one of these elite women who God continues to caress, love, provide for and even become jealous over.

*God has allowed me to jump into my sea of forgetfulness to pull out a few pebbles of my life to write about. From being **Fatherless** to being **Established**, I have been kept, first by men and their lack of commitment to me to finally seeing that I was always kept by God and His loyal love. I use to be ashamed of who I was. Now I share it with the world to help women understand their Godly position in Him. I am **A Kept Woman**, the daughter of James Tiller, Sr. and an intimate lover of Jesus Christ This is my story.*

Lynnette Tiller Appling

A Kept Woman

I've seen tears she cried
Watched pain in each sigh
Children in wonderment
Not knowing why
I've watched bills pile up
Saw what others ignored
Food supply short
No boats at shore

Yet she stayed on her knees
In the Word of God she believed
There's something the outside world could not see
She's a kept woman

Nights were long
But inside was a song
She couldn't give up on
The promises of God
Always knew He cared
Wouldn't leave her in despair
Gave her peace
In each heartache, He shared

He kept her mind and her soul
Woke her up and made her whole
He kissed her heart and
Restored her joy
He kept her
God kept her
She's a kept woman.

Lyrics from A Kept Woman
From Within: Psalms of Lament
Lynnette Tiller Appling
©2002 L.T.A. Productions

Epoch 1

Lynnette Tiller Appling

A Kept Woman

...And the arms of the fatherless have been broken.
Job 22:9 KJV

A father of the fatherless, and a judge of the widows, is God in his holy habitation.
Psalms 68:5 KJV

Lynnette Tiller Appling

Fatherless

I remember waiting so patiently on the couch for him to return. It didn't matter that it was 2 o'clock in the morning. At age four, I would turn on the TV, watch the *Nite Owl Theatre* and wait, sometimes falling asleep, for him to come through the front door. Finally, like so many times before he would stumble in. I would smell a strange smell upon his breath and wonder what could possibly keep him out all night and what kind of water was he drinking. I guess that question didn't matter much when I saw his face.

Daddy would come quietly to the couch, pick me up and hold me in his arms. "Why do you love me so much?" he would sometimes ask. I never answered. Somehow all the stumbling he did went away after he looked into my eyes.

We would have so much fun when he was around. Oh how he loved me. I was the apple of his eye and the only girl who could turn his head. I didn't care I had to share him with my mom as long as he came home to me. That's all that mattered. It wasn't long before the truth hit home. Yes, my home. The only true truth there was. I found out I shared him with not only my mother, but also some strange figure that I'd seen in the car. That night was a long one, one I will never forget. You see, that night I became different. I became *Fatherless*.

It was around 9:00 at night. I don't remember the date. My daddy came home early. This time was different. He didn't look at me or come to hold me like he normally would. I heard him and mother arguing and yelling throughout the house. I watched petrified as he packed up his bags and took his things out to the car. My heart began to throb as my mind began to ask questions. "This can't be happening to me, to us. What is he doing?

Doesn't he know how much I love him? Isn't he happy with me?"

My thoughts grew desperate as he walked out of the door. My mother followed him with my baby sister in her arms. She was just a few months old. I wrapped my arms around mommy's legs and held on tight. I didn't understand what was going on, but I knew my life the way it use to be was over. A few choice words were spoken between my dad and my mother. As they were arguing, I looked into the car and saw someone sitting on the passenger's side. I was so confused. "Who is this person and why is she with my daddy?" I thought to myself.

Suddenly, I heard his voice. "Nette Raye", he said so sympathetically, "Do you want to go with me or stay with your mother?"

What? What kind of question was this? I was four years old and you wanted me to choose between the two people I love the most? I looked him in the eye with tears flooding down my face and asked "Daddy, don't you love me anymore?" He answered, "Baby, I will never stop loving you but Daddy can't live here anymore."

At that moment, I felt the pain of my mother come from her heart to my soul. I looked up into her eyes, so broken, so hurt. I knew what I had to do. "I can't leave my mommy," I said. "Someone has to love her, someone has to take care of her Daddy." He smiled at me as if it were a relief to not have to carry the burden and guilt of leaving me. "Good-bye baby" he said.

Then he walked around his car and opened the door. He took one last look at what he was leaving and closed the door behind him. I will never forget the squeaking sound of the door. I counted the seconds it took to shut. "One, two..." I heard the key being turned and the motor of the car roaring like a lion. The sound of the car's motor rumbled in my heart and I took in a deep breath. "Twenty-five, twenty-six..." I whispered. He was gone. I buried my head into my mother's legs and began to say within my heart, "He'll be back at 2 o'clock in the morning. He always comes back".

The Path

My grandparents lived right next door to us. We quietly and slowly walked to their house. It was as if time stood still. I believe this particular walk was the longest walk of my life. Mommy didn't say a word, my baby sister was asleep and I could not help but wonder. My thoughts started to reminisce about each moment in time I had with Dad and how in a few seconds it was over. My tears seemed endless.

Everyone was at grandma's house. This seemed to be the norm. Somehow they knew something was amiss. The family surrounded my mother and began to talk to her. I must admit she held her head up high and no one really knew what happened until some time later.

The children who were my age asked a lot of questions. "What happened? Is he coming back?" they would ask. Not knowing exactly how to answer them, I would shrug my shoulders and put my head down in shame. Instantaneously, I realized I was no longer like them. They had a father. Their moments would never stop and stay frozen in time. I was so thrown and broken and now marked as a *Fatherless Child*. The stigma stunk. Tears rolled down my face burning holes in my cheeks as I realized... I'm not the same.

For years I walked around in this state, torn and teased. Derelict because the foundation I believed to be solid was shattered. Frayed because I was split in two. Who was I? Was I still his daughter or am I my mother's daughter? Should I continue to love my father, or will I be disloyal to my mother in hoping for his return? I was afraid of living life without him. My identity was gone. Of course the teasing did not help my mental psyche. Jimmy Tiller, Jr. my relatives called me. Normally, I would be proud of this statement, but I knew it was said to remind me that I was *fatherless*, *unloved* and *unwanted*. I was different from them. Set apart. An outcast. I could see myself separated in my mind. Though they were right there in front of me I was an outsider looking through the windows of their life, praying to be invited back in.

I was no longer special to anyone. Even the man who named me and charted my destiny by bringing me into this world walked away from me. The title of princess no longer applied to my life. I didn't feel like I had any worth and was constantly reminded that I was *Jimmy Tiller's daughter*. With this statement came the understanding that I did not belong to anyone, or anyone's family. Though I had a home, I was homeless. I was destined to make his mistakes and purposed to be like him. Not finishing anything, not loving anyone enough to be committed. This was my inheritance. This was my future. My family spoke his name not with respect or love, but with the knowledge that I, Lynnette Raye Tiller was Jimmy Tiller's daughter.

The smell of being fatherless continued to follow me throughout my life. I searched endlessly for the feeling of rest, peace and love I had with my father. There was security in his arms. But after his departure nothing seemed to fill the void. I even searched for him but to no avail. I asked family to help me get in contact with him, but to protect me they lied about were he was.

And so it began, walking in the steps he had so carefully laid out before me. They weren't hard to find. They were clearly marked and there were people who didn't mind helping me find them along the way.

With this search for my identity, I looked to my family for help, particularly my mother. At the time I did not understand that she needed the same help. Her world was shaken and turned upside down. I could just imagine the mental anguish and rejection she felt. Of course, at age four, there was no way for me to know this. I was dependent upon her and she was dependent upon Dad. We were both too wrapped up in our own pain, that we neglected to see the others. Daddy's carelessness and selfishness destroyed the women of my house. That night I lost both of my parents. Who would have thought one person had the key and the power to change the destiny of all of us.

This pain led to many crossroads between my mother and myself. I write this not to cause more pain, but to gain revelation and healing in an area, which needs much of both.

My mother was so beautiful. I remember looking at pictures of her before that dreadful night. There were actually smiles upon her face. At age 18, she was already employed and carrying her own weight in the world. She knew who she was and walked tall in it. In this respect, I am a lot like her.

I watched my mother struggle after Daddy's great departure. There were nights I heard her cry herself to sleep. There were no more smiles on her face, just regret. My mother could not possibly help me understand, because she did not understand herself. All she knew was somehow she had to survive this. She became the *man* of the family. Because of this something died inside her. The side that was so gentle became harsh and the warrior who could withstand anything moved to the back of her mind as the survival techniques came out. I knew of this well, for I too was doing the same thing. I was walking the same road with my mother, yet we were not walking together. This caused many problems in our relationship. The storm, which should have brought us together, tore us apart. I did not know her anymore. I craved her love, her words, and her touch. I felt I was a burden to her. I thought if I could just relieve her of me, she would do so much better.

I could sense the weight of the world on her shoulders. If I could only help her. Taking the stand I did with Dad made me believe she was now my responsibility. I was obligated to take the place of Dad. I didn't know there was no way to do this, all I knew was my mommy was hurting and I wanted to stop the pain.

So here we both were, ruined, cast down and carrying the same stench. She had no covering and neither did I. Both in love with the same man, both at the same crossroads of life and neither one of us understanding or seeing the other.

Some of the most hurtful words came out of her mouth towards me. Nevertheless, looking back I realize she was not talking to me, she was aiming her anger at the reflection of Dad. Out of all of the children, I am the most like him. I knew that every time she looked at me she saw him. I was a constant, irritating and painful reminder of my father.

"You're just like your father," she would often say to me. She had no idea how crippling these words made me feel. All I could think about was leaving, either physically or spiritually, I was getting out of there. There were many suicide ventures and many attempts of mentally removing myself from her and this life. I became rebellious and stubborn for this was the only way to keep the pain of the world out of my inner most being. Unfortunately my mother became one of the crucial people who pointed me in the direction of my father's footsteps. "You've always played the victim," she would say. Not understanding that, yes I was the victim and so was she. We were both victims of Satan's cruel plan to destroy us both with one blow.

Now let me interrupt to explain one vital point. I wrote this section not to point blame at anyone but to help women understand that Satan uses devices to destroy our seed. Sometimes as mothers we unwillingly and unknowingly tend to help him. We must break this bondage of hiding the dirty secrets that need to be exposed and begin to hear the voice of the Lord in situations where men abandon women. The children we birth are not our own, but gifts to be given back to God. Yes, not all women know who God is and do not understand this. Nevertheless, even in this point, to view any child we have as a mistake or to willingly give them over to our own pain is a tragedy. With or without the knowledge of who God is, woman must uphold their children as vital and precious assets to the world. They are a part of us. True, it takes two, a man and a woman, to create them. But see the half that is you and please stop destroying your children.

At the time of this unfortunate but true part of my life my mother was unsaved. This does not excuse what happened. She raised me according to what she knew at the time. I have forgiven her for this and she has forgiven me. Though at times we clash, today she is a strong force in my life. What she taught me in the early part of my life is vital to help you today. Now back to the story.

There were some family members who were not exempt from showing me the way to my father's footsteps. There were a couple of aunts who got their kicks by reminding me of the fact that I was inferior to them. I had many moments of tears and shame, some seen and countless unseen. My mother, sister and I were not rich. As a matter of fact, we were poor but you couldn't tell us that. We believed everyone went through the same things we did. There were days when the electricity and gas were off. During these times we would stay at our grandmother's house. Regrettably this didn't make things better. The circumstances in our life embedded more deeply in my mind the *Substandard Syndrome*. I wanted what my grandparents had. They had each other, their children and the love. I desperately desired their family lifestyle. Because of this, their house became home for me.

I almost forgot about the church, you know the wonderful, godly, sanctified saints. There was one church in particular in Chillicothe, Ohio that really showed me the way. When we first arrived at this church, I was so happy because of the many young people. I thought I would be able to lose myself amongst the many personalities. I just knew this was the place for me. As time went on, I heard the snickering behind my back. I was being teased and set up in so many crazy ways. There were no set incidents that were crossroads, but all of them combined created a road. I just kept thinking to myself that when I turn 18 years old, I would show everyone. I was going to come back rich and rub it in their faces. I would have my full revenge.

I couldn't sing at that time, nonetheless I loved music. I was constantly writing poems and songs, while plucking notes out on a keyboard my grandfather bought for me. One day I was singing at the top of my lungs in the church. It had nothing to do with anyone, just God and me. Every child in there including the adults cracked up. I vowed to never sing again. God must have heard me though. One day the leader of the children's choir got laryngitis and could not sing. The only other person who knew the words to the song was me. The choir director really did not want me to lead the song but had no choice. Finally it came time to sing the song. I walked up to the microphone and let out a note that must have had angels personally escort it to heaven. That's all I remember. Somehow, I left myself and someone else came in. They say I brought down the house. I have been singing every since.

The Butterfly

Let me back up about four years which would make me about six years old. I began to have dreams of someone bigger than myself, visions of someone walking with me. I heard about Jesus through Vacation Bible School at a Baptist Church in Circleville, Ohio, but never really knew Him. I was being taught a lot of religion, but something was lacking. So I began to look for Him myself and searched the skies in hopes of seeing His feet. I just knew He was riding on one of those huge clouds waiting to burst out. Maybe just maybe, He would take me with Him, just swoop me up, and the pain I felt would be no more. He made Himself known to me in a childlike manner. The wind would blow when I asked Him if He was there. When I asked Him if He loved me, the sun would shine brightly.

One day I was lying on the picnic table in Smith Park, crying over the fact that my aunts just threw water on me for having on new clothes. I wanted to die. They wouldn't miss me anyways I thought, begging Jesus to just take me. "Take me right now Lord!" I would scream. Before I could get the scream out in full lung capacity, a multi-colored butterfly came and sat on my hand. It wasn't afraid of me and it stayed on my hand for about five minutes. I was able to touch and caress the butterfly without it flying away. The beauty of the butterfly calmed me. The mere fact it would stay on someone as ugly as me wiped my tears away. Smiling at it, I understood that God was with me all along. At age six, it was enough to know someone loved me enough to send nature to hold me.

Today I often wonder about the butterfly and what it must have gone through in order to get to me that day. What awesome love God had for me to send a butterfly my way. The paths it traveled as a caterpillar, where it must have cocooned to be safe and finally escaping out of its shell, tranforming into a beautiful butterfly, just to allow me to hold it. Little did I know this was the beginning of my story. Not until later in life did I understand the significagance of the butterfly or its purpose. You see I too was a butterfly... I just didn't have my wings yet.

Lynnette Tiller Appling

A Kept Woman

The Fugitive

*(fyu'je tiv)
n. 1. Person who is fleeing or who has fled from danger,
or an enemy
adj. 2. Exile; refugee, fleeing or having fled, runaway or
passing swiftly; fleeting; 3. Moving from place to place;
roaming

Lynnette Tiller Appling

I am nineteen years old and now living on a bench on Livingston Avenue in Columbus, Ohio. I did it. I ran away from everything I knew. How did I get here you are probably asking? Take my hand as I lead you on the road of my past...

Running

My father was a very sick man. He was diagnosed with MS, a crippling disease that has made it very hard for him to move around or take care of himself. His fourth wife and I did not get along because I saw the filthy and deplorable conditions she hadmy father living in. Oh if I could take us back to that moment fifteen years ago and rewrite the script, he would not be in this situation. I knew I had to help him, so I moved in with him. He was hungry and getting skinnier by the moment. He really did not believe he was sick. He would still drive and try to fix cars. God forbid we take away his motorcycle. I enjoyed this time with him but in spite of this, my thoughts were constantly wondering how did it get to this point.

Well, Dad wanted to be a dad. I am not going to say I was a saint, because I was far from it. I had a boyfriend and I wanted to spend time with him. One day I got home around 2 o'clock in the morning. Maybe subconsciously I was reliving what Dad used to do and actually seeing it played out in front of his eyes must have angered him. It was our first real argument, and boy did I let him have it. "You don't come to my house late at night!" he yelled. "You are still my daughter and I have rules that you must abide by." I began to laugh hysterically at the irony of the situation. "Rules?" I said with a smart look. "Because I move in to take care of your black tail you actually have the nerve to try to lay down rules for me? You have no right to say anything about my life! I have raised myself for the last fifteen years without your guidance, your love or your fatherhood. Now... you have something to say? You abandoned your right to have an opinion when you walked out on me all those years ago! You, my loyal and committed father, have no voice to be heard!" I yelled at the top of my lungs.

I was so angry that I rushed upstairs and put all my things in a garbage bag. Then I hurriedly ran down the steps, gave him one last angry glare and slammed the door behind me. The anger and the pain elevated like fire in my soul. It continued to burn as I walked down Broad Street to Livingston Avenue. I became so hungry and worn out that I sat down for a while to rest. "How dare him," I thought with my lips poked out. "Rules, ha! You have got to be kidding me." I proclaimed. It began to rain outside. The coldness pierced my body and my soul. Another part of me died that night. Any hope I had for my father and me ended in that one moment. I had tremendous anger built up towards my father. Even at this age, the bruises of yesterday remained fresh and unhealed. I desperately wanted his love but refused to give him my love. Confusion overwhelmed me. Anger and hurt worked hand in hand to sustain me. Covering myself over with the trash bag, I started to remember my father's face. "I hurt him, I really hurt him," I said with mixed feelings. On one hand I didn't want to hurt my Dad, on the other hand, I felt he deserved it. Slowly, my mind drifted back to the anger and pain I felt when he left so many years ago. "Good! I thought. "He should feel the pain I've carried all these years." With this thought of rage digging an endless hole in my heart, I went to sleep.

Bleeding

The sun came up and the warm rays kissed my cheek as if Jesus Himself was waking me. My body was stiff and achy from sleeping on the bench. As I stretched out I suddenly began to realize what I had done. Panic terrorized my mind. "Where am I going to stay? What am I going to do?" I thought out loud. "I will never go home and I can't ever go back to Dad's". My stomach began to rumble from hunger. I searched my pockets to see if I had any change. Only lint came out. I looked to see if anyone was around to help me, but the people who were there looked as though they would kill me where I stood. I only had one option...call my grandmother.

The phone rang and her voice sounded so comforting across the phone lines. "Hello," she said. "If I could just see her," I thought. "Grandma," I said my voice shaking from tears. "Lynnette, where are you? I have been so worried? You need to come home." My grandparents were the only true foundation I knew. If I hurt any part of my body, she would be the one who I ran to. When I started my menstrual, though she told everyone, she was the one I asked for help. "Grandma, I need help," I said hopelessly. "Baby, tell me where you are and I will send Chee to come and get you". That's all it took. One call to my grandmother and she knew exactly what to do.

Chee came within thirty minutes. As we rode to her house in Columbus, the only thing she said was, "Clean up after you eat and lock the doors if you leave." She didn't ask any questions, instead she supplied a place of rest. She gave me money to buy a bus pass to get around Columbus. I knew it was now time to think about my life, what I wanted to do and how I wanted to do it.

I went to the downtown Lazarus and applied for a job. They hired me right away to work in the cosmetics department. This increased my self-esteem. I was making a little money and I thought I was grown. I dismissed the so-called boyfriend, because he was abusive. He was the type of man who wanted me to take care of him. He was lazy and lived off of me for far too long.

There was one time when we went to his mother's house while she was at work. He was acting kind of goofy and tripped over his own feet. I started to laugh so hard I almost wet on myself. Abruptly, I felt a piercing hit across my head. He had picked up a tuna fish can and was pounding me on the head. I jumped up and began to fight back. I knocked him to the bed and said, "Don't go to sleep. You better not close your eyes". Bruised, bewildered and angry, I went to the bathroom to wipe the blood off of my brow. I was stunned by the sudden turn of events. The girl in the mirror faded into the little girl that was lost so long ago. "Why are you allowing this to happen?" I asked the image in the mirror. "You have to love yourself". Slowly, I put my head down and turned on the faucet. Blood drops fell into the sink in slow motion. I took in a deep breath as I counted the drops, "Twenty five... twenty six..." Each drop that fell hammered the pain and memory of who I was deeper into my heart. As I counted the drops of blood, I said to myself, "I will never stop bleeding." I looked up to look deep within my own eyes. As the blood flowed down from the corner of my forehead to the edge of my mouth, I realized the inevitable truth of my existence... I was drowning in my own blood. "I will never stop bleeding," I whispered. Carefully, I wiped the blood from my forehead and gently wiped the corners of my mouth. Thinking of ways to get revenge, I tip toed back to the room and opened the squeaky door. There he was lying across the bed asleep. A wicked smile came upon my face. "I warned him," I thought. I scooted with my bottom down the steps to not wake him and went directly into the kitchen. "This will do," as I looked at the fine sharpened knife in my hand. Then I politely walked into the room and stretched my legs across his chest. Lightly kissing him on the neck, I began to strategically cut his throat. He woke in shock. He quickly grabbed his throat as if he already were dead. The cut was not a deep one, just enough to make him understand that I would kill him. He jumped up and began to yelp "You're Crazy!" I turned and looked him in the eye. Intense hatred swallowed up my whole being. I was tired of men and how they treated me. Laughing on the outside still bleeding on the inside, I walked down the steps and said, "Don't you ever touch me again. And by the way, lose my number".

Misplaced Trust

Lazarus was a place of much prestige. I was able to buy myself clothes and makeup. The people I met there were priceless. It was a typical day and there was nothing really special going on. I was in the men's department with one of my girlfriends looking at some things she was purchasing for her husband. While I was minding my own business a handsome older man caught my eye. I tried to be aloof but he was definitely looking at me. Because Lazarus was right downtown, some of my friends and I rode the bus to the Civic Center to eat lunch. I have never experienced the beauty of Columbus in this fashion. We casually strolled around the Civic Center. I was in awe of its beauty. I heard the piano softly playing in the background and began to sing the song that was being played. Singing, it was a long time since I've sung. I went to college to sing and got accepted with honors, but since those days my singing was somewhere left in yesterday. The music engulfed me as my voice rose higher and louder to the music. It was totally uplifting, so much so that I started to dance right there in public. Caught up in the music, I wasn't aware of the crowd that came around to watch. Once I opened my eyes, the crowd began to clap. I was so embarrassed by my actions that I began to hurriedly walk away. "What is your name?" a voice asked. I looked up and there was the same man who I had seen at Lazarus speaking to me. "My name is Lynnette", I said with a smile. His eyes were so friendly and kind. "May I buy you lunch?" he asked as he reached out his hand. "I think it would be nice". We laughed and talked and grew very fond of each other. That night he came and took me out to dinner. He came in a taxi *(this should have been my first clue)* to pick me up. What a romantic night it was. I went to a ball with him and danced the night away. He was seventeen years older than me but it didn't matter. What I didn't have with my father, I thought I had found with this man.

The Mistake

It wasn't long before we were married. We met in September of 1986 and married on January 24, 1987. There were problems right from the start. Minutes before we went to the courthouse to get our license, he proceeded to let me know he was married before. Now this should have been a warning sign. But of course, I ignored it. I enjoyed the touch and the attention of this man so much the secret did not matter.

I found out on a trip to Saint Louis in October of 1986 that

I was pregnant. I became increasingly sick during this trip. By the time we got back, I was experiencing the worst nausea I have ever had in my life. We began to plan our wedding for January. I had no dress and had to borrow one of my aunt's dresses. He wore a simple black suit. We couldn't afford rings so we bought each other a $19 gold band to wear. You see I was comfortable with this because struggle was all I knew. To me borrowing and being content with nothing was the norm.

I remember the wedding day. My aunts took me to Burger King on Main Street to get a Junior Bacon Cheeseburger. I was so hungry. As I was gobbled up the hamburger, my mind began to remember the night before. My soon to be husband stayed out till 2 o'clock in the morning claiming to be at his bachelor's party. The way he smelled and looked just wasn't right. I sensed something was wrong but refused to be alone. As a matter of fact, this wasn't the first time I knew something wasn't quite right. Earlier in October, before the pregnancy, women would come to the apartment and have arguments about me being there. He would rush them to the car and lie to me saying they were family members. He even lied about his own daughter and said she was his sister. It wasn't until she felt comfortable with me that she told the story of how she was adopted by her grandmother because her mother abandoned her. She also told me there were at least fourteen other children he had fathered. At the time, I believed she was only telling me this to get me out of his life. Another warning sign was now being ignored.

Our wedding day was cold and icy. I wouldn't let my father walk me down the aisle but instead had my grandfather escort me. There were roughly ten people there. Everything was borrowed and though it disturbed me, I refused to be denied. While I was slowly pulling the dress over my head, contemplating the reason why I was really going through with this marriage, my grandmother began to look through me to my soul. "Lynnette," she said with the utmost concern. "You don't have to get married. I know you are pregnant." I rushed to pull the dress over my head and turned to see her face. "A baby is no reason to get married. Besides, he is not your husband. I will help you raise the child. You don't have to marry out of fear or shame." She read right through me. But I didn't want my child to be fatherless. I just couldn't see any way out of this. My baby deserved to have a dad. Right then I wanted to run into my grandmother's arms and say, "Please take me away from here," but I didn't. Instead, I ignored my grandmother for the first time. With a small tear in the corner of my eye, I placed my veil on my head, pulled the lace over my face and remained silent. She knew. She knew way more than I could ever tell her or show her.

The ceremony was very brief and drama surrounded us. My new husband's father was a very abusive man and continued to abuse the man I married. I know this is one of the reasons why my husband could not show love, because he himself had been fatherless. His father was a rolling stone, wherever he laid his hat was his home and he made his wife miserable. Guns were used to manipulate and control his family. He and I did not get along, because I was not afraid or intimidated by him. I knew he was the essence of evil and I tried to help my husband's mother get free of him, not knowing that I myself was now married to a reflection of his very own creation.

My husband and I had a hard life. He was very selfish, uncaring and even cruel at times. As soon as he received papers on me, he acted out. Staying out all night, bills not being paid, no food to eat and of course he blamed me for his demise. He would say to me, "I wish I never met you" or "What did I possibly see in you?" I created and began to live in my own nightmare. I married a mirror image of my father.

My Angel

That summer was a hot one. There were some occasions the heat would hit close to one hundred degrees. My pregnancy had taken its toll on me. My legs were so swollen I could not see my feet. My weight went from 135 pounds to 162 pounds in just four weeks. I was sick with toxemia. My husband would always quit his jobs or get fired. Because of this, we didn't have insurance. This put my life in grave danger. I could not see my doctor on a regular basis. So, I saw him only one time before the day of delivery.

I was lying on the couch when a horrible pain shot through my back and down my legs. I began to take in deep quick breaths. "I think I'm in labor," I said panicking. My brother-in-law took one look at me, quickly called my husband at work and rushed me to the hospital. The pain was unbearable. I hated needles and all I thought the nurses wanted to do was stick me with a bunch of needles. My blood pressure went up to a dangerously high level and my head was pounding with intense pain. Because of this the doctors had to stop my labor and sedate me.

The next day the labor started again. Within six hours my only ray of sunshine to this nightmare was born on June 23, 1987 at 12:30 in the afternoon. Mansfield Malachi, IV. He was 6 pounds 5 ounces and 18 inches long with long coal black hair draped over his face. Unfortunately, I was still in great danger since the doctors could not get my blood pressure down. They whisked Malachi out of the room. I tried to keep my eyes focused on where the nurse was taking him, but they were too heavy to keep open. For days, I could not open them. Somehow, I knew I was dying. I was very weak and couldn't move any part of my body. I heard everything that was going on around me but I couldn't speak. The nurse thought I was sleeping. She had no idea I was dying. I wrestled within myself and said, "This is not the time to die." Trying to focus my thoughts and strength, I pushed over something that made a loud noise to get a nurse in the room. As she ran in to see what was wrong, I whispered with the last bit of strength I had, "Please help me!" She looked up at the IV and realized the medicine used to induce labor was still dripping into my blood stream. This medicine had been dripping into my veins for five days. It was killing me slowly. My doctor ran in and pulled the fluids from the stand and started regular fluids. Everyone rushed to wake me up and stabilize me. I heard the doctor holler at the nurse for being so careless with me. Within a couple of days I was well enough to hold my baby. To this day, I have never received a bill for Chi's delivery.

Malachi

Malachi was different from any other baby I had seen or experienced. He hardly ever cried. At such an early age he showed signs of being very smart. For instance, I would place him in his swing and give him a baby book to look at. He would literally turn the pages as if he could read. His smile would melt my heart.

Chi and I were the best of friends. He gave me so much purpose, so much life. He was the first one I ever watched the morning sunrise with. I would quickly wrap my son in a blanket and hold him close to my chest as I carried him outside. As I knelt down to sit on the step, he would turn and look at the sun coming up. His eyes got so big and full. It was if he knew where the sunrise came from. He was my life. Because of this, I desired to be a wonderful mother for him, however my circumstances dictated what I could and could not do. Yet, I dreamed and dreamed big. I would hold Chi and tell him all the wonderful things we were going to do together. How when he was older, mommy was going teach him how to sing. Every night I would sing and create wonderful songs for my son. It was easy to sing about him.

There were moments when he was sleeping, curled up and sucking on his little lip, that I would stare at him and praise God for such a miracle. I traced his entire body with my eyes. Methodically I examined his little tiny fingers as they curled around my pinky. I didn't understand everything about atoms and molecules, but what was lying on my chest was the most beautiful miracle of all.

I was breast-feeding my son to make sure he received the nutrients he needed only to find out I didn't have the ones I needed. My survival techniques came out. I would ask anyone for money to buy my son some milk and diapers. My husband spent his money on his women instead of providing for his family. I knew he was extremely jealous of his son. The way he would look at Malachi and acted around him made me not want to leave Chi in his care. Chi would cry every time he heard his father's voice and calm himself when he saw me. Our lives as a family was warped, but every time I looked at my son, my thoughts became clear and precise. In spite of our conditions at the moment, there was no denying the love my son and I had for each other.

It was time for Chi to be christened. He was the first grandson of my mother and the first great grandson of my grandparents. The date was set and I informed my grandparents and my mother of the time and place of the christening.

My grandfather was the head deacon of his church and my mother was an evangelist. They both had responsibilities to uphold in the church. I asked my mother what time she would be arriving to witness the christening of her grandson. She answered with a shocking response. "My place is in the pulpit". This statement went through my heart like a piercing dagger. Anger heaved in my spirit and resentment started once again. I truly did not understand why she could not be there for Chi or me. I made a declaration in my mind to never walk in her footsteps, for surely God would want her with me, by my side, as my mother.

At the church, I saw my grandparents walk in. I was so pleased to see them and they were so proud of their great grandson. My grandfather boasted so much I thought his chest would explode. As the minister began to touch the tiny little forehead of Malachi, he removed his hand in a backward motion and looked deeply into my eyes. "He is already blessed," he said. "God has done this before you requested it." My mind began to think back at what the doctor told me when I was well enough to go home. "Did you drink a lot of water during your pregnancy?" He asked inquisitively. "No," I said, "Why do you ask?" The doctor looked at me as if I was hiding some type of secret. "Because I've never seen anything like this before. Malachi had no blood on him at all. He was perfectly clean. Most children come out with a veil over their face and with mucus and blood. Chi came out with nothing on his body. He must be a special baby". Now hearing the words of the minister I understood and said to myself "Yes he is a very special baby."

The Death

My body began to change. I was frail and tired. I knew without going to the doctor I was pregnant again. This couldn't be happening so soon. Malachi was only four months old. I would be cheating him out of time with me and this so called husband of mine didn't know how to be a husband or a father and really didn't want to be either. "Lord," I cried out and looked up to the heavens, "I know I've caused this whole situation, but help me, please. I am so very tired and alone. Please, help me".

The next day I had to go to work. I begged my husband to drive me there, but he claimed he had no gas. "I guess not since you were running all over Columbus late last night," I said angrily.

I caught the bus and counted my last bit of money for the day. I wouldn't be able to eat lunch and I didn't have enough money to get home. I would have to walk. I began to estimate the miles it took to get back to where I lived and planned my day accordingly. I wasn't feeling well at all when I arrived at work. My head was dizzy and my temperature was rising. I made it till lunchtime and asked my supervisor if it was okay if I went home early. I called home to see if my husband could come downtown to pick me up. I explained to him what was going on, but he began to complain about the house being dirty and how he had to wash clothes and dishes. Chi was crying in the background and I knew he was neglecting him. I hung the phone up and in a rage began to walk home. It took me three hours to get there, but I did. I climbed the stairs, opened the door and collapsed. Blood was dripping down my legs. I could barely talk. My husband came to the door, made some smart remarks and told me he was going out with his friends. "You better have this house done when I get back!" he yelled. He politely walked over me and left. I crawled over to the couch and pulled myself up. Chi was in the swing looking at me. Somehow he knew I was sick. I slept for I don't know how long. Chi never made a sound. Finally, my husband came home. His friend was with him and rushed over to me. A puddle of blood filled the cushion of the couch. His friend picked me up and said to my husband, "Are you crazy man? She needs a doctor". It must have angered him to hear his friend show concern for me. He had to perpetrate some form of love for me so his friend wouldn't think less of him. So they both put me in the car and rushed me to Grant Hospital. "You have lost your baby". The doctor said. "There is nothing we can do. Take these antibiotics and rest. We will see you in a week to check and make sure everything is okay".

I went home and stayed in bed. Seven days went by. There were days I was better, but for the most part I was in a fragile state. It was now Wednesday, November 18, 1987. For some reason, I couldn't pull myself together. I just kept sleeping and sleeping. I would wake to see Chi laying beside me smiling, and gazing at me. I was breast-feeding so he fed himself whenever he was hungry. I called his father at work to ask if he could come home because I was not strong enough to care for my son. He cussed at me on the phone. "You are going to cost me everything. I wish I never met you". I've heard this statement so much in the past year I had grown numb to it. He finally arrived. I told him to leave Chi in the room with me, but he proceeded to tell me that if he was coming home to take care of this kid and me, then Chi would have to be in the living room with him. I was too weak to fight him about it. Chi screamed and cried because he wanted to stay with me. Just then, I heard a tapping on the window. There was a bird pecking to get in. The pecking calmed me. I closed my eyes and fell asleep to the sound of the pecks. When I awoke, I was tremendously better. However I couldn't feel my son's presence. Cautiously, I walked out to the living room and asked my husband, "Is Chi alive?" I don't know how I knew or why I asked. As I walked closer to my husband, I felt increasingly empty. I could feel my own heartbeat slow its rhythm with each step I took. He looked at me strangely and replied, "What kind of question is that?" As if he knew, he rushed to the couch and there Chi was... lifeless. I screamed, "Oh My God! Not my son, not my baby!" Falling to my knees, I started to crawl towards the front door. I pushed my way out of the house and fell down the cold cement steps. The Domino's manager across the street saw me and ran quickly towards my apartment. The landlord heard the outburst and without hesitation picked my baby up and brought him to his office to perform mouth to mouth.

I watched as they worked to make him breathe. Each puff I puffed with them. My heart began to slowly stop as I watched them blow each puff. The ambulance finally arrived. I took in one final deep breath. *"One, two..."* I counted the seconds. They tried to shock him back to me, *"Twenty-five...twenty six."* No more breaths. My baby was gone.

I was in shock. I couldn't believe it. I was lost and filled with a sense of void. I went deep within myself to escape the inevitable reality of not ever seeing, kissing or holding my child again. Rocking back and forth, I rolled in a small ball like a zombie, completely gone. All I wanted to do was hold my baby. I didn't want to hear what anyone had to say. I didn't want to know about how sorry everyone was. Just give me my baby. I walked over to where they placed his cold, limp body and kissed his cheeks. My tears tried so hard to warm his face. "Open your eyes for Mommy", I said. "Please Chi, open your eyes. It's Mommy. Don't leave me, baby. Don't leave your Mommy." With one last kiss, I touched my son's lips and gently shut his eyes. Little by little, inch-by-inch, I tenderly moved my fingertips over his face, sketching his small frame with my mind while permanently implanting his essence in my soul.

The landlord called my family to inform them of Chi's death. When they arrived my grandmother held me tightly in her arms as I continued to rock back and forth. The rocking back and forth ironically symbolized my life. At moments tipping into the past, trying to exist in the present, never really going anywhere, just rocking, sitting, and dying. This rocking motion in my life was now the only true existence I had. If I were to stop rocking, I would forever be stuck between yesterday and today. Nothing comforted me. My mind was leaving me. My spirit was crushed. The depths of my despair grew into a bottomless black pit. This was my resting place and I didn't want to come out. I began to decorate my new home with the memories of my son, frozen in the picture frames of time.

The Funeral

It was Saturday, November 21, 1987, Chi's funeral. As I walked in to Wayne T. Lee Funeral Home, I was amazed at the number of people Chi had touched in just four months. There had to be at least two hundred people at the funeral. Even my father was there. As I came up the aisle, I looked around the room. Both grandmothers were sitting on the front row. My mother had planned the whole funeral for there was no way I could do it and for this, I was deeply grateful. Slowly, I looked down the middle aisle to Chi's casket. I walked closer until I finally arrived at his side. "This is not my baby," I said bewildered. "Where is my baby?" People began to look at me as if they understood, but no one understood. I searched the room to see if anyone saw the pictures in my picture frames, but there was no one. I slowly placed the books and toys he loved in the casket with him. I couldn't walk away. The service began and I was still standing by the casket. "Why did they start? Let me have my time with my son" I thought. "All of you have cheated me for years, this is my time with my child and I refuse to let you steal it!" my thoughts shouted. I walked very motionless to the place where I was supposed to sit. My father's mother grabbed my arm and said, "You'll have more". It was so shallow, so meaningless. Is that all that she could say? Her grandson is dead.

As I sat down and gazed as the casket that now held my son instead of me, I began to outline his face in my mind. I did not want to forget anything about him, his smile, his touch the way he held on to my finger. I wanted to freeze the frames of his life in my heart.

The song *Jesus Loves Me* was being sung. This was the very song I would sing to him every night before he went to sleep. I blocked out the preacher. No one knew my son. Everything was just mere words being spoken. They were hollow to me. Just then, in the middle of my thoughts, someone fiercely grabbed me back into the moment. "I have a word for you from the Lord." she said. And before I could respond she abruptly put her hands upon my womb and said "God said, three more shall come, and nothing will be able to take them, hurt them or keep them from the divine destiny He has for them. Be encouraged for weeping shall endure for a night but joy cometh in the morning." I pushed her hand angrily off of my stomach, and with tears streaming down my face like a violent storm I said to her "I don't want three other children, I want my Malachi. Tell your God to bring back my son". She smiled as though not shaken or stirred by my words. I rushed to my son's casket and whispered, "I just want my baby back."

Breathing Again

The following Thursday was Thanksgiving Day. It was cold, dreary and raining. I found myself walking in the rain trying to find my way to Chi's gravesite. "He must be cold, I need to cover him." "Someone needs to help me dig him out of the hole, he can't breathe..." These thoughts, emotions and feelings overwhelmed and cluttered my mind. I couldn't grab hold of reality.

My mind and heart progressively roamed to the memories of my son. I knew I had no one now. Each day was a struggle to even live. The heaviness I felt plagued my very demeanor. To lift my head took extreme planning and practice. The ability to eat became a hardship and a handicap. It took a great effort to live, to wake, to take a bath and even to talk. To open my mouth and form one word, hurt. I would call my grandmother and cry sometimes not saying anything, just tears. She would listen and comfort me. She explained to me how one of her children died. Searching for some small form of hope, I would ask, "Could you breathe, grandmother?" "Eventually." She spoke with a definite conclusion. "Every breath led to another, until finally, I didn't need oxygen or life support anymore".

That same night I went to sleep. I had been having strange dreams about Chi. There were times in my dreams, I would hold him in plain sight and no one would see him. In other dreams I would leave him with a family member only to come back and find that they have no idea where they left him. However, on this particular night, when I fell asleep something extraordinary happened.

In my dream I was walking down a black narrow passageway, yet I wasn't afraid. Curiously, I kept walking towards a bright blinding sunray. The brightness of the light made me put my arms up to cover my eyes. As I continued, I took a step forward and stepped down onto a fleshly surface. Cautious of my surroundings, I began to look around and realized I was walking into the palm of someone's hand. I was literally walking up the middle finger. "This couldn't be happening," I thought as I felt my foot deepen into the creases of the finger. Turning I walked towards the middle palm of the hand and saw a very small figure. There sitting right in the midst of the hand was Malachi. All my concerns left me as I ran to pick him up. I was so happy and content. There were so many things I wanted to say to him. I twirled around in circles and pressed him deeply into my chest. I took deep sniffs to smell him. He was real all right. I felt the warmth of his body flow into the dead parts of my heart.

Not wanting to leave him, I turned and bellowed out with intense delight mixed with pain, "Please, I beg you, let me stay here with my son. There is no need for me to go back now. I am not wanted or needed." The voice, so gently said, "Lynnette, you must return for I have great works for you to do. I wanted you to know that Malachi is in the palm of my hand and so are you. I love you so very much." Tears overwhelmed my whole body as I tried one more time to plead my case "My Lord", I begged, "Please, Please..." Just then, I felt a mighty and strong wind. My body became limp as the wind picked me up and turned me towards the tunnel. Feeling the breath of the Lord breathed into me, I openly received His love. I didn't fight what He wanted to do and surrendered to His will. His breath became my breath and with one split moment, I was back.

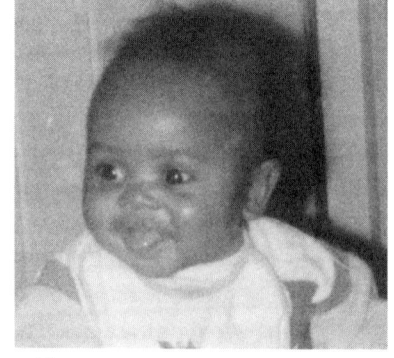

From that day on I have never mourned my son with despair or had dreams about him again. I remember, but the pain that came with the memory, is not a part of the picture frame anymore, only his smile.

Shaila, Joshua and Garra

It wasn't long before I was craving to have another child. I desired so much to hold a baby close to me. If I could just have one more chance, I would do a better job at being a mother. I went to the doctor believing I was pregnant only to find out that I wasn't. The doctor informed me I would probably never be able to have another child. He explained to me that because of the deaths of both of my children so close together my mind had shut down my body. It literally stopped producing estrogen. Refusing to believe what he was saying, I thought about what the woman said at Chi's funeral and about the dream. I knew if God was truly real then I would have my children. The doctor looked into the use of fertility pills. He believed this was the best way to go. I was to come back in one week to begin the process of taking the pills.

At this time, my husband and I decided we needed to get away to just rest. So we packed up our bags and started to go to Geauga Lake. It had been a long time since we actually smiled at one another. In a way, I think he was glad I wasn't in the black pit anymore. These were some of the rare and far between moments I saw and experienced the tender side of him. I do believe he loved me, but because of the pain he had growing up with his own father, he really didn't know how to love. I knew without any doubt I loved him. I believed my love could change him.

We pulled into a McDonald's when intense heat went through my entire body. I became grossly ill. Nausea, pain, rapid heartbeat, and fever came upon me all at once. My husband quickly carried me to the car and drove ferociously down I-71 South to Grant Hospital. Once there, they rushed me into the Emergency Room, started an IV and began to run blood tests. "Is there any chance that you could be pregnant?" the attending doctor asked. "I just saw my doctor and he told me I wasn't." I stated as I began to fall asleep. I really don't remember how long I was sleeping, but I do remember when the doctor came back into the room.

"Congratulations", he said, "You're pregnant." "What?" I didn't care about the IV's, I forgot about my fever and jumped straight up and replied "You're kidding, right?" "No," he said, "I'm not. Make an appointment with your doctor on Monday, drink plenty of fluids and get some rest". I laughed uncontrollably. Immediately, the dream came back to me and I remembered what the voice of the Lord said "You are in the palm of My hand". I started to remember the course of the dream and for the first time, I understood. Finally, I realized I could never heal from the loss of Chi because I refused to truly believe he was gone. I was holding on so tightly that it was slowly killing me. God had mercy on me and then showed me kindness by relieving me of my own self-induced hell. He welcomed me into His presence to explain that I was not alone. When He breathed His life into me, healing took place in my mind, my heart and my soul. At this moment of revelation came a sense of newness for my life.

I did have my three children just like the woman said. Each one of the children was born in a time of my life when there was nothing but turmoil. Nevertheless, they gave me such incredible hope and courage. No longer could I live for just me. Here is the miracle: there were no menstrual cycles in between any of my children. From the time Chi died till the time Garra Lyne' was born, not one menstrual. It puzzled my doctor, still, he delivered each miracle. My children became my life. They are what created passion in me. According to the doctors and specialist, these three children were not supposed to be born. It was medically impossible, so they thought.

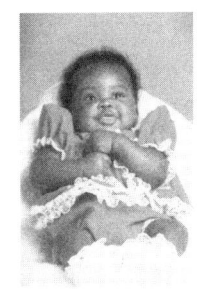

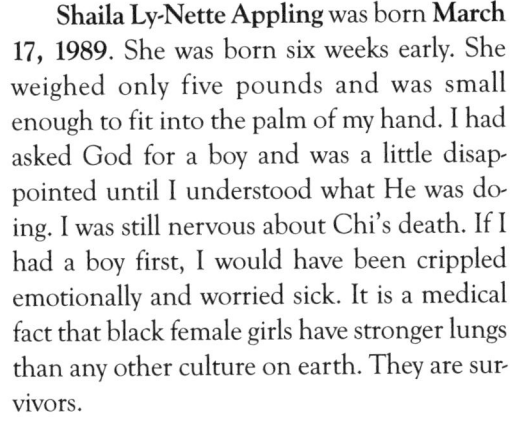

Shaila Ly-Nette Appling was born **March 17, 1989**. She was born six weeks early. She weighed only five pounds and was small enough to fit into the palm of my hand. I had asked God for a boy and was a little disappointed until I understood what He was doing. I was still nervous about Chi's death. If I had a boy first, I would have been crippled emotionally and worried sick. It is a medical fact that black female girls have stronger lungs than any other culture on earth. They are survivors.

Shaila was diagnosed with a spinal disease, which would cause serious damage to the brain. The doctor said she would be paralyzed. However, God said she would walk. Shaila is a basketball star and a dancer. She enjoys having fun. She is my comedian and my joy. Today, Shaila is very saved and loves the Lord.

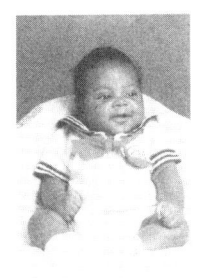

Joshua Forte' Appling was born **June 8, 1990**. It was a tough pregnancy for me because he tried to come in the twenty-fifth week of pregnancy. I was hospitalized for over two months and stayed in and out of the hospital the entire pregnancy. He was my promised one. Today, he is very anointed. He sings, preaches, draws, sketches and loves the Lord with all of his heart. He wasn't supposed to make it but was born at six pounds and two ounces. I named him in honor of his great-grandfather Forrest Lowe, Sr. He is my blessing.

Garra Lyne' Appling was born on **October 3, 1992.** Garra's birth was unique and special because she was born in the same hospital just two floors down from her great-grandfather Forrest Lowe. I believe he waited until she came before he went home to be with the Lord. Garra is her grandmother Paula Tiller, her aunt Mary Tiller Woods, her great-grandmother Gretchen Lowe and me all wrapped up in a neat little package. She is my princess. Today, she is the president of her student council, has started a Bible study in her school, and enjoys crocheting, cooking, dancing and singing. Oh, did I tell you she is a tremendous joy in my life?

Because of my three wonderful children, the running away had to stop. I had to learn to face my ultimate enemy and conquer my greatest fear. My only problem was... how do you face off with yourself?

A Kept Woman

Lynnette Tiller Appling

Deep Wounds

For my iniquities have gone over my head. As a heavy burden, they are too heavy for me. My wounds are loathsome and corrupt, because of my foolishness.

I am pained and bowed down greatly. I go mourning all the daylong, for my body is filled with burning. There is no soundness in my flesh. I am faint and severely bruised. I have groaned by reason of the anguish in my heart. Lord, all my desire is before You. My sorrow is not kept a secret from You. My heart goes out in pain, my strength fails me. My lovers and my friends stand aloof from my plague. They also seek after my life and lay snares.

Those who seek my hurt speak mischievous things and meditate deceits all day long. For in you, Oh Lord, is my hope. You will answer. For I am ready to fall. My pain is continually before me. I will declare my iniquity.

I will be sorry for my sin.

Psalms 38:5-20 ASV

Lynnette Tiller Appling

I truly wish I could end this story right here and make it seem as though my life was just wonderful. I wish I could say that once I experienced God face to face and felt His breath inside my lungs that I changed immediately and walked right. But, I can't. Even through all of that, God still wasn't enough for me and losing my son still didn't jolt a deep change in my spirit. I didn't learn the consequences for my actions or my disobedience. Instead, I chose the road, which brought more anguish, more pain, identity loss and incredible heartache. Let me introduce you to my open wounds named *"Abuse and Terror"*. Follow me...

Revelation

My husband now had the ability and the authority to fool me. I gave him complete power over my mind and my soul. On one of his periods of being absent from the family, which most of the time lasted for months, I was lying face up on my bed. There was no food in the house, the gas was off and I had three small children to take care of. I began to come in tune with the pain that erupted out of my soul. Ferociously grabbing my chest, I pressed my hands into my heart as the shower of tears took over. I took a well-needed journey into my soul. Memories flooded my mind of every heartache and every moment he abandoned the kids and me. Just the day before, I was washing rugs with my bare hands and hanging them on the clothesline. With no money to purchase pampers, I was forced to cut up my last few bath towels to use as diapers for my children. I had to depend upon the children's pediatrician at Children's Hospital to write a prescription to purchase milk for my children. Because there was no gas in the house, I had to set buckets of water outside on the back step and use the rays of the sun to warm the water for my children's bath. Selling all of the furniture in the house was the only option I had to try to keep my children and I from going hungry. We ate off the floor of the apartment. I even sold our clothes to pay the electric bill. "Where are the children of God? Why am I suffering this way?" My heart pounded so hard I thought I was having a heart attack. "I can't do this anymore. I can't walk six miles to the grocery store pushing the children in a stroller and having no one to help me. I can't sleep by candlelight one more night. I can't stand the silence anymore. I just can't." The peace once dwelling within emptied through the pores of my entire body. "I can't... I can't.... I can't.... give up," I bawled. Silence at once filled the room. There were no more tears. Not one could be pushed out. Hearing one of the children crying, I didn't move. I couldn't move. There was nothing I could do but lay still. Once again, God made His presence known to me. When I opened my eyes there was a drawing of two roads crossing in the center of my ceiling. One was wide, while the other was narrow. Thinking I was hallucinating, I squeezed my eyes shut to see if it would go away. I opened them again to find the same drawing looking down upon me. I heard His voice say to me "Choose the road you want to travel." Pondering the statement, I asked Him, "Lord, where is my husband?" He responded, "Which road do you want to walk on...the narrow or the broad?" I answered Him and asked "Which road leads me to the truth?" He said, "The one walked with me". "Then this is the road I will travel Lord," I said. He responded by saying "Go to the back of your car, there in the trunk is the truth you have been seeking." I jumped up from the bed, made sure the children were okay and ran out the back door to the car. I quickly opened the back of the trunk and there it was just like the Lord said; love letters from a fourteen year-old girl to my husband containing intimate conversations between them. There were undergarments still filled with their intimate encounters, booklets of different hotels where they had stayed, our bank statements of the money he took from our account, along with the receipts of how he spent the money on her. Now it made total sense, all the bacterial infections and diseases I had to get treated for. His numerous affairs almost cost me my children's lives. It was all there. The truth. I almost fainted. The truth felt like a giant punch to my lungs. I couldn't breathe. I knew but didn't want to face it. Even my best friend tried to tell me and I didn't believe her. I wanted so desperately to believe the best of him. Marriage meant so much to me. I tried so hard to have what my grandparents had. I didn't want this marriage to end like my parents. Yet, this was the path I was on. I was now at the very moment and place my mother was in so long ago. My heart felt like it was going to explode.

I stumbled to my neighbors apartment walking like I was drunk. I asked her if I could use her phone to call my mother-in-law. I finally figured out the phone number and clumsily dialed it. "He's been cheating on me," I said trying to catch my breath in between words. "Well, you know men do this kind of thing," she replied. I was so surprised and appalled by her response that I hung the phone up on her. I went back to my apartment and rocked on the couch. "I hate him with everything in me". That's all I could say. I checked on my children and looked upon their faces to calm me down. "I must live for them now" I reflected as I walked slowly into the bathroom to wash my face. Reaching for the towel, I caught a glimpse of myself in the mirror. Succumbing to my fate, I said to myself, "You will never stop bleeding". Right away something grabbed me from within. I pushed my shoulders back, took another look at the mirror and said out loud to my reflection, "Today you will". At that moment I heard a knocking at my door. No one ever came to see me so I was curious to see who it was. Lo and behold it was my mother-in-law. She apologized and informed me that my husband, her son, had been meeting the girl at her house and she had allowed him to use her address for their love letter exchange. I shook my head in disbelief. I could have taken this hit if I didn't love this woman, but it just so happened I did love her. I really believed and thought we were friends. Walking past her, I opened the door and escorted her out of my house. As if that wasn't enough, guess who came home for dinner after being absent for over two months? You guessed it.

Boy, did I laugh at the irony of the situation. Little did he know the truth was out. I waited patiently as he opened the screen door. Yes, I'm telling you right. He had the nerve to think he could just come in and take a shower with no explanation or apologies. But that day he met his match. I had been broken for far too long. Struggling in ways that were at times barbarous. Because of this, from somewhere deep inside me came strength of a thousand strongmen. I watched and plotted carefully, as he placed one foot on the floor and then the other inside the door. Just then, I pounced like a female bear. Filled with intense anger and pain, I grabbed him by his throat and picked him up off the floor. Squeezing his throat as hard as I could, I ran down the list of everything I found. Every pain, every memory, every tear became the strength I needed to continue strangling him. He was scared and I saw the fear in his eyes. Out of shock, he stumbled with his words. "No one will ever want you. You will never make it without me". As I released him from my grip, laughter rumbled in my spirit. I laughed hysterically as I told him how he just signed his life away by having these affairs. His words had no affect on me because the pain that he bestowed upon me during our marriage had already damaged my heart. I walked closer and closer to him as he leaned his back up against the door. With my teeth grinding and penetrating snarl, I commanded him to take his old crusty, nasty, disgusting, self out of my house and never come back again. He ran out of the apartment like a wounded dog. For just a few moments I got satisfaction. At the time, I didn't know this was a spirit I was fighting. I can't despise the man, but the spirit in the man. He's never known the Lord as his savior. Again, this does not excuse his behavior, but I do forgive it. Today I pray for his salvation.

Emptiness

I'm going to jump forward a couple of years and pull back the curtain to a particular stage. On this stage is a young lady with three small children, which has now

A Kept Woman

moved on hoping to find some peace and rest in her life. This is where this act begins...

Trying to provide for my children, I was forced to move into the ghetto area of town so I could afford the rent. It was a small apartment with two bedrooms, a very diminutive kitchen, a feeble likeness to a dining room and a marginal living room. I made the best out of the situation and decorated this little apartment as though it was a mansion. Frequently, I shopped *The Dollar Store* exquisitely pronounced *Thee Dollae Storea* and somehow furnished this apartment to make it feel and seem like a wonderful place to live. I went from being an assistant manager at several retail stores, to a part time bank teller, to an on-site apartment cleaner, in other words, a ghetto maid. That's right. I scrubbed toilets in the ghetto to take care of my children. During this time I met a handsome young man. At first, he said all the right things and did all the great things. I fell head over heels in love with him to where I neglected myself and believed solely in him. It was him and me against the world and I stayed with him on and off for almost seven years.

It all started so innocently. We met, we dated and we fell in love. I should have looked deeper into his eyes to see his soul. Little did I know I was sleeping with the enemy. This man was custom created by Satan himself for my complete destruction and I didn't know it. I was caught off guard and caught looking for love, searching for my purpose and broken from life. I was vulnerable and didn't know who I was. My trust and belief in this man was to the point where I allowed him to alienate me from my family, my church, and at times, my children. I desired to be loved so much, that I allowed another person to have access to my innermost self without regards or respect for my children and myself. I freely gave up my identity without any fear of the consequences. When he spoke, I listened. Whatever he wanted, I did or tried to do. In my mind the thinking pattern was, if I could please him, he would never hurt me or leave me. My good works would make him into the man that I desired. However, he was never satisfied. He was self centered, cruel, manipulative, distorted, selfish, and egotistical. He thought he could come to my job and act like a fool whenever he felt like it. I became his property. I could not have thoughts of my own. If I would express a dream, it had to be within the confines of his order and rule. I became a wooden puppet, afraid of being human, yet too wooden to cut the strings of terror.

No one liked him. Not my uncles, not my aunts, not my church friends and not my children. He had a perverted mind and made me do vulgar, disgusting, degrading, humiliating things in order to *keep him happy*. He dangled marriage in front of me, bought me a huge diamond ring, showed me the receipt to prove that it was real and then told me I wasn't ready. I really didn't know exactly when or how, but I had to find a way out of this relationship.

I wanted more out of life and more for my children. I didn't want to be on welfare anymore, and I truly did not want to be with this man all my life. I sought the Lord's face again. "I know I am not worthy and the lifestyle I have chosen is not what you want for me, but in spite of what man says on earth, I believe You can hear me. If so, show me what to do in order to be what you desire for me. If I am a lost cause then allow me and my children to leave this world today." I didn't really know how to pray. However, I knew God was real and the only way to get out of any of this was with His help. Within two days God answered me and said "Lynnette, I want you to learn of Me" "But how can I learn of You when I don't understand Your hard-to-read Bible." I did not say this to be smart or disrespectful, but I couldn't read the King James Version at all and I wanted understanding. He said "Go to the bookstore and I will lead you to the Bible that will help you to understand. Realize, I can't help if you do not act." Now what you need to know is that even though I strayed quite a few times, I was raised up in the church and knew a little something about the Word of God. I took the basics of what I was taught and applied them, but only like Burger King. In other words, I only asked Him when I needed Him. I wanted it my way.

I went to the Christian Armory in Columbus, Ohio on Kimberly Parkway. I was a little nervous about what I was going to

A Kept Woman

find. "Where are You Lord" I whispered, "I'm at the store like You said." Right then the Lord said, "Go to the Bible section and there you will find a gray Bible that will be easy for you to read and understand". Sure enough, there it was and it was on sale. I put my last few dollars together and bought the Bible.

I started to read it from the beginning and researched it. I started to understand a little about who I was and how God viewed me. It was nothing like this young man, who claimed to be saved, sanctified and full of the Holy Spirit, said I was.

My thought process slowly but surely began to change and though I was still weak in a lot of areas, there was something happening on the inside that refused to be denied. The wooden puppet became human. With this newfound life, I reached up to cut the strings.

Suddenly, I didn't want this man touching my body or violating me anymore. His pleasure was not my concern. I started to hang up the phone when he called me and that's when the nightmare began. The phone would ring every five seconds like clockwork until the morning hours. The phone company, at my request, disconnected my phone. When I would go to work he was waiting for me. One particular incident I had some church friends over to my apartment. He saw my lights were on, went to a pay phone and called to see what I was doing. Because I knew he was crazy, I would lie and tell him nothing. Within minutes I would hear scratching at my door because he would stoop down to listen to find out who was at my apartment. If he heard any voices he would bang on the door, wake up the neighbors and scare off my friends. I couldn't breathe. I became frightened of his irrational behavior. His stalking spirit was in full display.

One evening when I chose not to answer the door, he banged on it for so long that I finally opened it. I don't know why I did. Maybe so my kids could get some sleep or maybe I thought I could talk some sense into him. When I saw his eyes, I realized it was not love that consumed him but something more powerful. I really believed I was face to face with a demon from hell. He pushed the door open further, grabbed me around my arms and violently threw me into my glass dining room table. Anger overtook me and I got up and started to push him back. Without warning, he hit me as hard as he could in my face. As I fell to the floor holding my face, I watched as his rage got out of hand. Without any regard for my children or my things, he viciously destroyed my apartment and my most precious intimate mementos of my family. All of Malachi's pictures were destroyed. The jewelry box from my grandmother was broken into a million pieces. Trying to get a reaction, he watched me closely as he thrashed the plants from each one of their gravesites to the floor. I gasped and watched in horror. Slowly I rose from the floor and stood tall in front of him. I turned and looked at everything he destroyed. Without fear, I looked him in the eye and stared him down. I could see the bewilderment in his eyes. It amazed him to see the new strength I had. With anger drenching his heart, he started to grit his teeth tightly together and spewed, "You are nothing but a whore with three kids. There is no one who wants a used, tore down hoochie momma. I don't love you. There is no one who loves you, even your ex-husband didn't want you." My knees started to buckle but I refused to give him the satisfaction of seeing me hurt. Without warning my mouth opened and said, "I do not need a man to love me for God is all the love I need." As soon as I spoke this out of my mouth, he reached up and punched a huge hole in my wall. "Be glad this isn't you," he said and walked out of the apartment. Just then my knees lost the strength to stand and I fell to the floor. I thanked God for sparing my life and for keeping my children asleep.

Every day after that became a challenge to move forward. On one hand, I was reading the Word of God, on the other hand this man made it his life's mission to torment me. I was completely torn by my feelings for him and my new desire and thirst for God.

This man had become part of my lifestyle. There were some days I wouldn't hear from him and because I was so used to drama, I became uncomfortable with the silence. It was like an addiction. I know what you're thinking. Why didn't you call the police? Well I did. But because I was black and lived in the ghetto, I was treated as though I deserved everything that happened to me. There was absolutely nowhere for me to go. What about the church? At this particular time in my life, I was attending the church my mother and grandparents attended. I was going through the motions. Though I experienced God, I didn't truly accept Him into my heart. I knew the rules of what not to do and what I could do. This was taught very well in the church. Here was the struggle. Rules! Do this. Don't do this. You're going to hell for acting this way. My relationship with the church was all about rules. Their law could not quench my thirst for revelation nor could it keep me saved. That's the other thing... I was baptized at four years old and filled with the Holy Spirit at age ten yet, I was sitting on a church bench and dying. Life and people were silently and strategically killing me. The church, which was to be a place of refuge, became a place of confusion and distrust. If I told anyone, and I did, the problems became common knowledge from the pulpit and all my fault. There were no solutions or answers for real life problems. Abuse wasn't talked about in the church, the true definition of marriage wasn't defined, and mercy and forgiveness of love was never explained.

I learned all about Johnny Walker (for years I thought this was a person) and Sister Organist and what she did the night before, but I didn't learn anything about principles or the never-ending love of Christ. I was doomed and going straight to hell according to the church. A backslider sliding right out the back door. Here is the crazy part, I was singing in the choir, head youth usher and shouting on Sunday morning.

Masks were easy to wear then. Let's see, there was one mask for the church folks, you know, the *Hiding Mask*. "How are you Sister Tiller?" one sister would ask. "Blessed by the best," would be my response. There were a couple of masks for my family, the *I'm Strong and Can Handle Anything Mask* and the *I'm Prosperous and Pulling It Together Mask*. And yes, even one for my children, the *Don't Worry, Mommy is Going To Make Everything Okay Mask*. Don't forget the one for the job, the *I'm Intelligent, Don't Mess*

With Me Mask. Oh, please don't act like you don't know what I'm talking about because even right now as you are reading this you are maybe wearing a mask, you know, the *Self Righteous Mask.* The one that says, *I Would Never...* or the *How Could You Allow...*or better yet, the *That Couldn't Possibly...* Please, don't fool yourself. We all have layers and some of them stink. Up until now, the church was not smelling or wanting to sniff out my layers, let alone pull them back. There was nothing they could do for me or for anyone else for that matter.

So, I continuously went through my own hell. The terror became a best friend to me. It attached itself and went everywhere I went. My emotions, my self worth, and my ability to comprehend love, went out the door. Still, I wanted peace. I wanted to rest, but didn't know how or even where I could find this rest.

In searching for this place, which seemed unobtainable to reach or find, I had an idea. It seemed like the only alternative at the time. I would take the lives of my children and myself. I couldn't leave them behind knowing their course of life was already set in place like it was for me. I packed them up in the van, turned on the engine and drove motionless to a railroad crossing. I waited patiently for a train to come. "As soon as I hear one," I thought, "I would thrust my van in front of it. This way we would not feel any pain." As I sat waiting for the train, so many thoughts went through my mind. Memories of the past few years played like a movie on a giant screen in my heart. I had to accept the responsibility of my choices. Yes, I had a rough beginning, but somehow I had to get through this. I kept looking and searching for the train. It had always been on time. Strangely, the train never came and I grew tired of waiting for death. Slowly, I turned the van around and looked at my sleeping children. "This is not what they deserve," I whispered. Still, my wounds went too deep and seemed impossible to heal. From the abandonment of my father, to having my own children abandoned by their father, I had truly been walking on the set path my father made ahead of me. I was repeating the cycle, wishing my wounds would turn into scars, but they were still opened. So opened that the young man dug deep into the old wounds and made sure they did not heal. He didn't use salt, he used his words, his actions and even the Word of God to keep digging deeper into my open sores. Everything that happened permeated my bones. They were a penetrating living part of me. Every word, every thought, every violation of my body, every hit, every infringement of my spirit and each moment of pain, would remain with me forever. I knew I would never stop bleeding naturally and spiritually. Eventually, this loss of blood would leave me empty and lifeless, leading to my death.

Lynnette Tiller Appling

A Kept Woman

The Covenant

*1. A solemn agreement between two or more persons or groups to do or not a to do a certain thing. 2. A formal agreement that is legal
3. The solemn promises of God to man; compact between God and man.

Lynnette Tiller Appling

A Kept Woman

Learning To Trust

I was running very late for my temp job and somehow had to find enough time to pick up my food stamps. I looked at my watch and started to plan. I dressed and fed my children, ran out of the house, dropped them off at the daycare and proceeded around the corner to the food stamp office. "Please Lord, don't let there be a line. I only have twenty minutes to spare," I thought to myself. As I pulled around the corner, sure enough there was a line. Frustrated, I quickly parked my car and rushed to the next space before the other person got there. Impatiently, I waited and kept glancing at my watch to see how much time I still had. It was then the Lord spoke to me. "Get out of the line Lynnette, you don't belong here." "I know that wasn't God," I said to myself "and it surely wasn't me". I looked around the line at the people. There were some there who truly needed the stamps, but there were others who were driving brand new cars. There were men smoking cigars, waiting for their women to come out of the building all doing mighty fine from what I could see. I knew about the scams some of them did with the selling of the food stamps for fifty cents on the dollar. I watched and grew solemn in my spirit. "Get out of the line Lynnette," the voice said again. "But Lord, how will I take care of my children, what will they eat?" I didn't say it out loud but whispered it quietly in my heart. He replied, "Trust Me." I looked around one more time, walked out of my place and got in the car and drove to work. Once I was there the Lord spoke to me again. "Lynnette, call your caseworker and tell her to take you off welfare." "What Lord!" I asked almost out loud in a screaming format. "I trust you but that is a great big step for me!" "Trust Me," He replied. I couldn't believe it. I was dialing the number and began to tell my caseworker to close my file and take me out of the system. "Please keep my children on the insurance and the daycare allowance but take me off of the rest." I said in total bafflement of my own words. "Are you sure you want to do this Lynnette?" she asked "Maybe you should pick up your food stamps for this month and I will take you out for next month."

"No", I said, "I know you probably won't believe this but God told me to do this." "Okay, Lynnette, but if you change your mind, give me a call." I hung the phone up with so many questions in my heart but I did not voice them. I had been reading the Bible and learning about the Israelites and how God brought them out. This is what I wanted... total and complete deliverance.

I got off work and picked up my children. I checked the apartment grounds before getting out of my car to make sure the young man wasn't around to stop me from getting into my house. I rushed upstairs with the children and told them "Kids, today, we are off welfare". They clapped, but I am pretty sure they didn't know what they were clapping about. At their age, anything that made Mommy happy, made them happy. Hearing their applauses raptured something in my spirit and joy came to me. I started to clap with them and sing. Wanting to celebrate with my children, I took out the last package of chicken, a can of green beans, a box of macaroni and cheese, a box of Jiffy cornbread and made us a celebration meal. Afterwards, my children and I curled up on the couch to watch some well deserved cartoons. What a peaceful moment. I loved and cherished them so much. Any hard day I had seemed to melt away when I was with them.

After putting them to bed, I began to wonder about how I was going to feed my children. I knew they would get breakfast and lunch at head start and the day care, but what about dinner? All I could think about was what God had said...trust Him. "Well Lord," I said "Your move." And with that thought went to sleep.

It was Saturday and time to wash clothes, wash the children's hair and normally buy groceries. Twenty-five dollars was all I had to do everything including putting gas in the car. As I was wondering how to separate this money, a knock came to the door. I looked out the peephole to make sure it wasn't the demon from hell. Seeing a familiar face, I quickly opened the door and asked, "What are you doing here?" It was a friend who owned a meat market. He said, "I was talking to my wife and

A Kept Woman

she told me to bring you and your kids some meat. So I brought you a two weeks supply of meat and vegetables to help you out." As he brought in the food, I started to cry. I couldn't believe it. God kept His promise to me. So I took out fifteen dollars of the money to keep in a safe place for gas and used seven dollars and fifty cents to wash clothes and paid two dollars and fifty cents for tithes. I wanted to thank God for keeping His promise. This must have activated the keys to heaven, because on Monday I received a phone call from my temp agency telling me a design firm needed a receptionist right away. I was three hours late for the interview due to someone locking away my clothes at the other temp job I was on. Anyway, I arrived at Chute Gerdeman and boy did I look a mess. Somehow, I got the temp position. After only two weeks the owners hired me permanently. At first, they started me out at eighteen thousand dollars a year. I was so grateful to Denny and Elle just for that. This was in October. By February they gave me a raise and began to pay me twenty-one thousand dollars a year. Within two years they raised my salary to twenty-four thousand dollars a year. God directed my steps and used Chute Gerdeman to be a blessing to me. I began to see the hand of God activated in my life. God allowed me to have favor with the owners of the company. Denny began to teach me about excellence and tutor me in business. Elle instilled in me how to have taste and class. I loved them both so much and I knew they loved me. I experienced life through new eyes.

During this time, I left the church of my mother and grandparents and searched for a place to really call home. The more God dated me, the more I wanted of Him.

I remembered the church my sister attended. I knew I didn't have the clothes or the looks to fit in, but I didn't care. The name of the church was New Covenant Believers under the guidance of Pastor Howard Tillman. This is when my life turned into the direction of purpose.

Finding True Love

As soon as I walked in the church doors, I instantly knew this was my new home. I didn't know anyone there and they didn't know me, which was actually good. Because of this, I was able to concentrate on my healing and not on what others thought about me. It was truly adventurous to go to this church without family or support, but after everything I had been through, I was up to the challenge. At this point of my life, I was truly desperate for a change. The young man was still harassing me, my heart was completely shattered beyond recognition and it was scattered all over Columbus, Ohio.

The first thing I heard when I walked in the door was the worship. It was not like anything I had ever heard before. I actually felt something stir up in my spirit. It wasn't about who could sing the best or who was there or even Johnny Walker. They were humbly stepping into the Presence of the Lord. I carefully examined how everyone was out of their own self, not caring about who saw them or what opinion one may have of them. I could sense the Presence of the Lord inhabited this house of worship.

After worship it was offering time. Now this would be the real test. If they began to get up and go to the bathroom during this time, or if they walked around and just touched the basket as if someone owed them something, then this church was just like all the others. I scooted up to the edge of my seat to get a better view of their faces. To my surprise there was joy, clapping, dancing, and singing. I sat back and smiled. "Truly these people enjoy the love of God," I thought.

"Now for the next test," I said to myself. "If this preacher starts talking about Johnny Walkers and Sister Organist going to hell, I will walk out." Everyone stood with their Bibles opened and read the Scripture out loud. Pastor Tillman came up to the pulpit, which in itself shocked me. Why wasn't he sitting up high in the pulpit like all the other preachers do? He was different. He sat with his people on the front row. Not only was he sitting with the people, but he was also approachable. This led me to think he didn't want all the glory nor was he more than the church. The impression he gave me from this one move was like us, he makes mistakes and like the church he must dwell in God's Presence. This was one of the first insights I received just sitting in the pew.

As he approached the podium, he began to speak. I actually understood what he was saying. The Word of God became alive. It was so simple and so good. My soul craved more. I started to come to every service not to socialize, but for the Word. For the first time, I didn't bore at the thought of the preacher coming to the podium but looked forward to the voice of God. I would take my Bible at home and begin to read it for myself in a more enlightened way. The words leaped up off the pages and captured my spirit. It was as if they were slow dancing with me, holding me, loving me. It was alive and it was real.

Because of this, at work during lunchtime, I would walk down High Street in Columbus and have a conversation with the Lord without moving my lips. His spirit surrounded me. I was no longer afraid of tomorrow for I knew God was with me today. Not only did things change in the spiritual realm but manifested in the natural. I went from living in the projects to living in a brand new three bedroom, three-bathroom town home. Because of Child Support being increased, my salary went from just twelve hundred dollars a year to thirty two thousand a year. I bought and paid off my own washer and dryer. I was able to purchase a new van without a co-signer. Money seemed to just show up in the mail and on my job. One time in particular, my old Honda needed a new transmission. It cost over eight hundred dollars to get it fixed. I didn't know what I was going to do. Within two days, my boss passed out bonus checks to all of his employees. Just like that, I had the money to get the car fixed. These are the kind of things God did for me. After I moved out of the projects and had only lived in my new apartment for six months, the Lord told me to check my mailbox. It was a Friday afternoon, and I had just gotten paid. I thought it was just me, but the voice got louder. I already had it planned on how to spend my paycheck in paying rent, buying groceries, you know... the usual. Finally, right when I got to my exit and almost passed it, I decided to listen to the voice. I pulled up to my mailbox and opened it up. I saw a gray and blue envelope and I knew by the appearance that it was my child support check for the kids. Slowly, I opened it up. I saw the first zero and thought, "That's nice, I got another hundred dollars to put with my regular paycheck to pay on some other bills." I kept on opening up the check and there was another zero then another zero, I quickly pulled off the rest and started to scream. The check was for three thousand dollars. I must have screamed extremely loud, because one of the neighbors pulled up to see if I was okay. I said "Girl, I just received a check from Child Support..." and before I could finish the rest she started to scream to. I stopped and looked at her as though she was crazy and asked "What are you screaming for?" She said, "If God can do it for you then I know my child support check will be here to." We both started to laugh uncontrollably. I picked up my children from daycare, paid all of my bills and had some left over to purchase some things for the house. I even opened up a checking account.

The next couple of weeks I was on cloud nine. My trust in God eluded all depths of understanding. I think because of this, God decided to make a personal appearance. It was around 8:00 pm on a cold and snowy Friday night in January. Winter in this particular year was very bad. I lived in Delaware, Ohio in Lewis Center and the snow would get so deep that if I would open my door, my living room would be covered with it. The children were all tucked in to their beds and I went into my master suite. Yeah, you read it right, I had a master suite with its own bathroom attached. I placed my Bible before me, pulled down the blinds and began to write a prayer for guidance.

Lord, I just want to be in Your Presence. Here I sit waiting on an answer from You. Wondering which way that You want me to go. I am alone and my enemies are great and at each turn. I feel them hovering around me like lions waiting to pounce on their prey.

Lord, I seek Your face, I request refuge. For I grow so tired. My sword needs sharpening and my helmet needs to be insulated. My armor is cracked and desperately calls for soldering. But God, I find no fault in You. Grant me restoration to You. Clean me up. Give me the water of Your belly. Let me rest my weary head upon Your chest. Breathe Your breath of life inside my nostrils, and place upon my heart Your blood stained hand. Give me life.

For You are all knowing and Your love far exceeds the limits of men. Your glance at any situation will destroy the enemies that are at my door. You have sent me to be a warrior unto the nation. You have created in me a mighty work. The songs of Judah You have embedded and fiercely stamped upon my tongue. The words of Paul and Peter You have plowed into my heart. Let not I faint in the battle for I am accountable to my Master. I cannot do anything without You. I am Your servant, I am Your clay, mold me.

I wrote this prayer and carried it with me until this very day. As I was writing, the very Presence of God filled the room. The words of the prayer came from my soul and my spirit and God knew that it was pure. Within moments, Jesus was there sitting on my bed with me. He said, "Pick up your Bible and read Isaiah 54 and every place that says Israel or makes a personal reference, put your name there. Everything that you read, I will do for you for this is My covenant with you. Never forget these words." I hastily turned the pages of my Bible to Isaiah 54 BET and this is what I read:

Let your voice be loud in song, O woman without children; make melody and sounds of joy, you who did not give birth: for the children of her who had no husband are more than those of the married wife, says the Lord.

Make wide the place of your tent, and let the curtains of your house be stretched out without limit: make your cords long, and your tent-pins strong.

I will make wide your limits on the right hand and on the left; and your seed will take the nations for a heritage, and make the waste towns full of people.

Have no fear Lynnette; for you will not be shamed or without hope: you will not be put to shame, for the shame of your earlier days will go out of your memory, and you will no longer keep in mind the sorrows of your widowed years.

For your Maker is your husband; the Lord of armies is his name: and the Holy One of Israel is He who takes up your cause; He will be named the God of all the earth. For the Lord has made you, Lynnette, come back to him, like a wife who has been sent away in grief of spirit; for one may not give up the wife of one's early days.

For a short time I gave you up; but with great mercies I will take you back again Lynnette. In overflowing wrath my face was veiled from you for a minute, but I will have pity on you forever, says the Lord who takes up your cause.

For this is like the days of Noah to me: for as I took an oath that the waters of Noah would never again go over the earth, so have I taken an oath with you that I will not again be angry with you, or say bitter words to you.

For the mountains may be taken away, and the hills be moved out of their places, but my love will not be taken from you Lynnette, or my agreement of peace broken, says the Lord, who has had mercy on you.

O troubled one, storm-crushed, uncomforted! See, your stones will be framed in fair colors, and your bases will be sapphires. I will make your towers of rubies, and your doors of carbuncles, and the wall round you will be of all sorts of beautiful stones.

And the Lord will make all your builders wise; and great will be the peace of your children. Lynnette, all your rights will be made certain to you: have no fear of evil, and destruction will not come near you.

See, they may be moved to war, but not by my authority: all those who come together to make an attack on you, will be broken against you. See, I have made the ironworker, blowing on the burning coals, and making the instrument of war by his work; and I have made the waster for destruction.

Lynnette, no instrument of war, which is formed against you, will be of any use; and every tongue, which says evil against you, will be judged false. This is your heritage Lynnette a servant of the Lord, and your righteousness comes from me, says the Lord."

That night the Lord had me read Proverbs 31 BET and this is what it said:

Who may make discovery of a woman of virtue? For her price is much higher than jewels. The heart of her husband has faith in her, and he will have profit in full measure. She does him good and not evil all the days of her life. She gets wool and linen, working at the business of her hands.

She is like the trading-ships, getting food from far away. She gets up while it is still night, and gives meat to her family, and their food to her servant-girls. After looking at a field with care, she gets it for a price, planting a vine-garden with the profit of her work. She puts a band of strength round her, and makes her arms strong. She sees that her marketing is of profit to her: her light does not go out by night. She puts her hands to the cloth-working rod, and her fingers take the wheel. Her hands are stretched out to the poor; yes, she is open-handed to those who are in need.

She has no fear of the snow for her family, for all those in her house are clothed in red. She makes for herself cushions of needlework; her clothing is fair linen and purple.

Her husband is a man of note in the public place, when he takes his seat among the responsible men of the land.

She makes linen robes and gets a price for them, and traders take her cloth bands for a price. Strength and self-respect are her clothing; she is facing the future with a smile. Her mouth is open to give out wisdom, and the law of mercy is on her tongue. She gives attention to the ways of her family; she does not take her food without working for it.

Her children get up and give her honor, and her husband gives her praise, saying, unnumbered women have done well, but you are better than all of them. Fair looks are a deceit, and a beautiful form is of no value; but a woman who has the fear of the Lord is to be praised. Give her credit for what her hands have made: let her be praised by her works in the public place.

He taught me about Himself. That night the Lord claimed me as His very own. He explained to me that I am a Proverbs woman, though I was used and abused by men, His righteousness has made me an honorable woman. He did not see me as man did, but He saw the blood of Jesus claim and cover me as His very own. In the book of Isaiah, He clarified of how He Himself would never treat me in the manner in which I have been treated by mankind. If Jesus was not going to say bitter words to me, than what right does mankind have to say it. He was the ultimate quintessence of love.

I wept as He caressed my spirit and soul with His loving Word. Every broken place was being mended. My lover, Jesus Christ, was sweet talking me into His Presence. He also showed me that I have a promise, a covenant with Him and I have had it since the beginning of time. He loved me so much that He came all the way from heaven to tell me I was beautiful in His eyes and what He placed in me from the beginning of time will be manifested. I became His and He became mine. There was no in-between. I was free. Free to love, free to sing, free to make mistakes without condemnation, but most importantly free to live. My search was over for the ultimate lover. He was my husband now, my provider, my guidance, my friend, my hope, my comforter and my mirror.

Jesus gave me a kiss that night and with the kiss came the breath of life. When I began to breathe, I did not have to count anymore, for His breath will never cease to fill my longing heart and soul. It wasn't a breath that just filled my lungs, but a breath that filled my spirit and mind. I could breathe in without fear and release breath without damnation. My grandmother was right. My life support has always been me trying to survive. Now with Jesus, life support is no longer needed for each breath I take is His breath sustaining me through every hurdle, every complication, the good times and the bad. There was peace in knowing I wasn't alone anymore. When I had a hard day I could talk to my husband about it. When the kids didn't understand the pain I was in, I could talk to my lover. I even talked to Him about my hair, my clothes, my bills, and my groceries. There was an incomprehensible knowledge of His complete involvement in my life.

He enlightened me to the incredible fact that because He already shed His blood to save me, my blood was stolen from me, unjustly, and illegally. The blood that came from the hits, and the bleeding that erupted out of my soul were not supposed to happen. Every time I would bleed internally or outwardly from my own mistakes or from the mistakes of others, it robbed Him of His glory and me of my inheritance. What inheritance am I talking about? My inheritance of peace, establishment, and victory. My blood was never meant to be shed, spiritually or naturally. He already completely and thoroughly finished this many years ago. I am not saying I don't have to go through anything, but I am saying I will no longer allow anyone to rob me of my blood given inheritance or my Savior of His glory.

By His stripes everything that caused emotional, spiritual, and physical wounds and scars are now declared healed. Just one touch was all I needed. Just one word was all I wanted. To know He loved me without any doubt conveyed to me peace and placed me in a position of rest.

Now it all made sense, my past, the moments of seeing Him, but not knowing or trusting Him. Still, He didn't give up on me. He kept on loving me. He just kept on loving me. Even when I didn't love myself, He kept on loving me. I held on to Him that night in a way that is unexplainable. My thoughts became renewed. I was new.

It didn't happen like the preacher said it should happen, nor did I have to be perfect. The teaching of, *I have to come to Him with my life together* was a bunch of bologna. He met me in the midst of my nightmare and brought light. Right when I couldn't move, think, or love, He became real. So to all of those preachers and teachers who say that can't happen…it did and it will continue to happen. Please, if you are like me, don't be afraid to call out to Him. It doesn't matter where you are or what you are doing, He will show up for you. I know this as a fact, for He showed up for me.

Because of this incredible encounter with Jesus, I was strong enough to join the choir at New Covenant. I placed my children in every child's program there was in the church and I even became one of the secretaries who helped out when needed. I began to live a life of promise and covenant. Now when I looked in the mirror, it wasn't drops of blood I saw, but the loyal unconditional love of God.

A Kept Woman

The Awakening

Now Peter and those who were with him were overcome with sleep: but when they were fully awake, they saw His glory ...
Luke 9:32 BET

See then that the time has come for you to be awake from sleep: for now is your salvation nearer than when you first had faith.
Romans 13:11 BET

Lynnette Tiller Appling

The Anointing

Many people couldn't understand the change in me. It was like night and day. I began to write songs and poems once again. One in particular went like this:

> *Lord I know I've failed You in so many ways,*
> *When life got hard I ran.*
> *I tried to do things my way.*
> *Lord, I know my flesh is weak*
> *In this I can't deny,*
> *But You have given me*
> *Everything I need to survive.*
> *Lord, when I look and see*
> *Just how much You loved me,*
> *In the midst of my adversity,*
> *You took such good care of me.*
> *Your awesome love I see,*
> *Your gentle touch I need.*
> *My soul can't explain it.*
> *I give my life to You.*
> *Why is there so much love,*
> *For a person such as I?*
> *You've proved Your faithfulness,*
> *Your love never dies.*
> *I feel Your arms,*
> *Wrapped around my soul.*
> *Your forgiveness I feel.*
> *The only gift I have*
> *Is to surrender up my will.*
> *Lord, when I look and see,*
> *Just how much You loved me,*
> *All I can do is give my life to You.*

Songs and words like this one continuously rolled off my tongue. I was in a love relationship no one could understand. My enemies at my job were removed. Even when the people talked about me, I couldn't hear the rumors. Nothing seemed to harm me. Yes, even the young man lost his affect on me. My awakening came when I was not expecting it or even knew what it was about. Let me explain.

This Sunday was like all the other Sundays when I went to church. However, the Spirit of God was on a much different and higher level. The people were praising God in a way which ushered you into His presence. The love in the church was very pungent and I knew God was touching me. I opened my mouth and called out upon His precious name. "Jesus," I whispered "Jesus, Jesus". Each time I called out His name, I could literally feel Him approaching me. I couldn't hear the music or the cries of the people anymore. It was just Him and I in the room. My intimate worship became an abiding place for Him. Unexpectedly, I found myself somewhere unfamiliar and new. I lifted my eyes to see where I was. There in front of me were His feet, His wonderful beautiful feet. Because of the glory I felt in front of me, I wouldn't or should I say couldn't, lift my eyes to view His face. I wept uncontrollably. I couldn't grasp why He loved me so much. It humbled me to a point of awareness of how awesome He truly is.

In that moment of worship, I felt a wet, warm, thick liquid substance flow from the top of my head and saturate my entire body. It had a very sweet, pleasant smell. I could sense from the way it flowed and engulfed my being that it was oil. Jesus was pouring oil on me. The oil was refreshing and calming. I didn't comprehend in that moment, what was happening or what it meant, but I did realize He was calling me and preparing me for ministry. After He poured the oil, He reached down to my face and placed His loving finger underneath my chin. I won't pretend or mislead you into believing I was calm. I wasn't anywhere near calm. My heart rushed and was beating beyond my chest cavity capacity. I thought my heart was going to expand out of my chest. I began to sweat in reverence of the almighty God. The mere power of His touch was unfathomable. I was speechless. When He touched my chin He tilted my face towards His. I couldn't see anything but light. Within milleseconds, I came to myself in the church spread out on the floor. Pastor Tillman was in the middle of his message. "How long was I lying here?" I thought. I couldn't explain what had just happened to me.

As soon as church was over, I rushed home and called my mother. I began to tell her about how I was transformed from one moment in time to another, and how Jesus anointed me. "Did He tell you what He was anointing you for?" my mother asked "No, and I didn't ask" I replied. I mean really, when God, Himself, the very essence of Him is touching you, do you think you will ask questions?

After my conversation with her, I laid across my bed and began to remember everything that had happened to me over the last two years. His hand was very prevalent in my life. Not one split second went by when He was not seeing, knowing and always intervening in my life. I didn't know why the anointing happened the way it did, however, I was excited about my relationship with Him. I turned over in my bed and turned off the light. With tears of joy I whispered, "Thank you Lord for such a wonderful, intimate experience with you. I can't predict nor will I try to explain what is going to happen next, but I am ready to walk with you. Whatever you want me to do, I will do. Wherever you want me to go, I will go. This is my covenant with you, and this time, I plan on keeping my promise."

Little did I know what was forthcoming in my journey. The anointing was just the beginning of my preparation for the road ahead. He awakened the new Lynnette and placed His name "Christ" beside my old name. He called out the gifts in me. The pouring of oil was just the beginning of where He was taking me. For the first time in my life, I wanted to be faithful, to have a commitment. My reward was not the titles or the fame, but was actually Jesus Christ. I sought out His face, His love, His wisdom, and His touch. In seeking only Him, all of the rest will follow. Instead of looking for who I was in man's eyes, I sought out Jesus' eyes. It was written in the Old Testament that no one could look upon Him and live, (Exodus 33:20) well, I didn't want to live, but desired that He would grow and live within me, to where there was no more Lynnette, but only Christ (Romans6). Because of this discovery, my heart craved to be more a reflection of Jesus and less a testimony of man.

A Kept Woman

Epoch 2

Lynnette Tiller Appling

A Kept Woman

My Boaz

And Naomi had a relation of her husband
A man of wealth...
And his name was BOAZ.
Ruth 2:1 BET

Preparation

It was February of 1999. I was in my new apartment writing and practicing for my first CD entitled From Within: Psalms of Lament. I opened up my heart entirely to music. As a child, I received many awards and competed on national levels against some of the nation's best. I was even on live recordings featuring the Honors Choir at Ohio Wesleyan University. But the long journey of my life sidetracked me and prompted me to put my musical aspirations on a dirty shelf somewhere deep within my soul. Joining the New Covenant Believers Choir stirred up that gift again. I thoroughly enjoyed singing and writing music. To help me focus on doing something positive, I began to research how to record a musical CD.

God sent some wonderful people into my life to help me write and create from my heart. The music was therapeutic. I wasn't singing or writing to be like anyone else, though many people thought this. I just wanted someone to be touched by the message that Jesus truly does care.

At the time, I didn't realize God was preparing me. He had me in His Word on a daily basis. I didn't miss a Bible Study class for I hungered after His Word and revelation. My job was going well. I was happy and content being where I was for a long time. I wasn't looking to be in a relationship with anyone but the Lord. I became so involved in my children's lives, their work in school and church, that I really didn't have time or room for games or people.

My children and I had a regular routine on Friday nights. To unwind from our hectic schedule, I would make homemade pizza and we would rent a Disney Movie to watch.

I also became very good with my money. In my possession was a brand new (at least it was new to me) Dodge Caravan. What you may not understand is because of my first marriage my credit was shot. The car I had was unreliable to say the least. I was on vacation, (thank God that I was), when the car totally broke down. I had no transportation at all. I prayed to my Provider and asked for wisdom on how to handle the situation.

Looking through a newspaper, right on the front page was an ad for a thousand dollar coupon to use as a down payment for the car of your choice. I asked a friend for a ride to the car establishment. I filled out the paperwork and waited for about ten minutes. The woman told me to go and pick out the car I needed. I was shocked. She didn't reveal to me the amount I was approved for, so I went out thinking and believing I had to settle for the worst vehicle on the lot. She looked at me and said, "Is this really what you need? I told you to pick out what you need." I walked back to the expensive cars. Looking past the small cars I went straight to the van section. I scanned the lot with a huge smile on my face. My eyes met the very van I fell in love with. It was a deep maroon color with maroon interior. It only had forty-two thousand miles on it and was in mint condition. The van was three years old. I looked at the woman with joy and said, "This is the one I need". She replied, "Very well, here are the keys. Come in and sign some final paper work and the van is yours to take home." Just like that the Lord gave me a new van.

Not only did He provide me with a new vehicle, but also I was able to buy two new bedroom suites and pay off one of them. This gave me a good credit standing at the furniture store and aligned me with the opportunity to purchase new leather furniture with all the trimmings. In addition, God had my mother's friend purchase an oak dining room suite for me. My family bought me towels and other household items to decorate my home. I was in very high spirits.

Budgeting became a privilege to me. I would budget out my groceries, my kid's clothes, gas and bills. However before all of this, I would pay my tithes and offerings. Because I remained faithful to what God had told me to do, He was more than faithful and full of mercy and grace towards me. It wasn't because of my works I was granted favor. It was because of my obedience to what He told me to do and for being a good steward over the very small items He put in my possession. I did not waste anything. Not money, not time, nor opportunities. Every dime, every second, every occasion was accounted for.

My children attended the most expensive daycare in Delaware County, not because it was expensive, but because God said I had rights to claim the land He gave me. They went on field trips, learned a different language and were properly prepared for school. The daycare became a second family to my children and me. God provided all the embellishments and accessories I would need to survive in this life. I was fulfilled with being Lynnette Tiller and living alone. I was complete. Yes, there were rare moments in which it would have been nice to have a saved girlfriend to talk to, but it never was like that for me. I noticed early on in life that even female friends were rare.

In the midst of this precious time of rest, God saw fit to bless me with my personal ***Boaz***. I really believe He was making sure the gift He would give me would be properly taken care of. He didn't want me to bring down the man He would provide. This was my preparation time to be at ease with who I was and work to improve myself. When I could properly manage His vineyards, which were my children, my home, my finances and my spiritual walk, then He could trust me.

Christ had to teach me how to cherish covenant relationship and abide by promise and commitment. I couldn't learn this from any man, but had to learn it sitting at the feet of Jesus. If this process of learning trust and commitment didn't take place, I would have destroyed the very gift He was presenting to me. I wasn't perfect, but I was obedient.

Meeting Jeff

It was Tuesday, April 12, 1999, at approximately 6:00 p.m. I just picked up my children and was treating them to Bob Evans on Polaris Road in Delaware, Ohio. It was there I met the man of my life, Jeffery Lyn Appling.

He was visiting his mother in Columbus, Ohio and stopped at Bob Evans to get something to eat. At first, I didn't think much about him, but he must have been thinking an awful lot about me.

I saw my seven-year-old daughter Garra winking at him and

making eye contact. She was flirting. I don't know when she learned this art form, but she was good at it. We began to talk and soon it led to laughter. My children were very comfortable with him and excited that he was with us.

I had plans to take my children to the park and asked Jeff if he would like to go with us. Of course he did. I watched him very carefully to make sure he wasn't part of the Shrek Syndrome. What is the Shrek Syndrome? It's when someone appears to be one thing and truthfully they are something else. Because of so many broken promises, and due to the fact my world was pretty much settled I didn't want anything to mess it up.

The park was very nice. There were a great deal of people there with their children. My children were so happy to be playing and jumping around. Jeff and I sat on one of the benches and began to talk. We talked about our beliefs and some of the pain we had experienced. He was so easy to talk to. Still, my guard was up. As any good mother, my eyes were on my children and Jeff at the same time. Jeff didn't try anything and his focus wasn't totally on me. He kept his eye on my children also. Every time I thought I saw something that might have been a moment of concern or danger for the children, he would react before I did. This made me consider his words.

He told me he lived in Canton, Ohio and was a schoolteacher. Well, this counted him out automatically because, I wasn't leaving my church and I had already told the Lord I was not moving anywhere up north. Delaware, Ohio was as far north as I was going to go. In spite of that, there was something soft about his eyes and sincere, so I kept on listening. I never felt so at ease with anyone, but my children. I was myself. No mask, no worries and no real concerns.

It was getting dark and Joshua said he had to use the restroom. I went to gather the girls and started towards the bathroom, but before I could take another step, Jeff had already escorted Joshua to the restroom and protected him. "This just doesn't happen," I said to myself. "Men's main motive is to try to get me to sleep with them. They have never cared about my children. But this man cares."

Looking down at my watch I decided the children needed to get some rest. I tucked them into the van and fastened their seatbelts. I turned to say good-bye to Jeff, but right before I could say anything he began to speak. "Lynnette, you and your children are what I have always wanted. This is what I want." I was blown away. I was a little intimidated and weary. I immediately began to think the worst and wanted to high tail it out of there. But my feet weren't moving. I stared at him deep within his eyes, trying to see his soul. I wanted to reach the innermost depths of him so he could understand what I was about to say. "You don't know me or my past" I responded almost in shame. He replied, "What I do know is what I want". This response was something God Himself would have said. Smiling at him, I accepted his words. He gave me a kiss on the cheek and helped me into the van. We exchanged numbers and made plans to see each other on the following weekend. He followed me long enough to get to the freeway and waved goodbye. The children screamed out the car like a well-trained choir, "Goodbye, Jeff!".

Confirmation

I must admit I was on cloud nine. However, I kept saying to myself, "He can't be real. Just wait Lynnette. The true Jeff will emerge. It always happens this way. You get yourself together and then you allow someone to come and mess it up. Don't even waste your breath or thoughts. End it now and you won't have to worry about heartache." I already made up my mind I was not worthy of such a commitment and I would sabotaged any attempts to love me. But God had another plan.

It wasn't a good two hours before the phone rang and it was Jeff. We laughed and talked for about five hours on the phone. I couldn't help but feel like a schoolgirl. In one night he met me and cared. He must have seen something I forgot was there. I have been so busy being a mom, a servant at the church, an employee at my job, that I almost forgot I was also a woman.

For the next few weeks, our relationship blossomed. We were inseparable. He took a few days off work and stayed in Columbus to spend time with me. We went out to dinner, lunch, breakfast, you name it. He swept me off my feet.

I was afraid to tell anyone about him because of my past. I knew how cruel people could be. The moment they see you prosperous in spirit, they remind you this was not their plan for you. Not everyone is happy when you're happy. For this small amount time, I wanted to enjoy the joy and not have anyone ruin it for me.

Somehow my little sister Mary sensed in the heavens the angels were rejoicing over our union. It wasn't long before she called to verify what was revealed to her. "Lynnette," she said after I picked up the phone. "What?" I replied. *"Why is the Lord telling me, Boaz?"* I began to shift my weight on my feet, searching my mind to find a way out from discussing this with her, when the Lord brought back to my memory of what I was studying just two weeks before I met Jeff. I was studying the book of Ruth. I tried to play it off, so I responded very calmly and smoothly, "I don't know, why don't you ask Him?" "I think you do know, Lynnette," she said, as only Mary can say things. I knew Mary would not get off the phone unless I told her, and since she knew anyway I might as well let her hear it from me. "Well, I met a wonderful man, who has all the traits and characteristics as Boaz. I have been praying to God to find out if he is real or not." I said casually as if it didn't matter. Mary replied, "Well I guess he is because God told me to tell you Boaz". "Please don't tell anyone yet Mary. I want to keep this my secret for a while. Besides, you know how family is?" I said, begging for her vow of silence. She agreed and got off the phone.

After the conversation with my sister, my doubts were laid to rest. I embraced my love for Jeff and rested in his love for me. I've never experienced unconditional love like this except through the arms of Jesus.

There was so much joy in my life. I would pack up my children and travel to Canton, Ohio to spend time with Jeff. To my amazement, my children were already calling him Daddy. He would personally take each child and love them one on one. He wanted them to know he would always be there for them.

Now it was time to announce our love to the world. Well at least to our family. This was particularly hard because both of our mothers knew the pain we've experienced in our past relationships. Jeff and I knew they might not be so accepting of this relationship since it was so soon after both Jeff and my past relationships. We decided the best time to do this was on Mother's Day. This would be a mutual place for us to let them know of our plans and then we could run quickly out the door if need be.

I invited my mother to dinner at Jeff's mother's house. Before I told my mother about Jeff, Jeff confided in his mother about me. She cried when he told her. Not because she didn't like me, but because she didn't want him to get hurt. I thought this was so loving. I understood her heart and did not take her response personally. She loved him so much that she felt his pain. I decided the best way for her to know I was sincere was to spend some quality time with her. So, I took her where I knew we could both be on common ground... I took her shopping. We had the best time. We laughed, we joked, and we spent money. She became one of my best friends. I didn't know women could be friends until I met her.

Mother's Day quickly approached. We had a wonderful time. I got to meet a lot of Jeff's aunts and enjoyed them so much. There was nothing phony about his family. The love was real. I could see why I loved him. He came from a very loving, close-knit family who knew who they were and where they were going. I basked in the love that day. But the day wasn't over. To my astonishment, Jeff announced to everyone that he was going to marry me. Finally, a man who truly went after what he wanted.

In my eyes, Jeff was a wonderful man. He didn't want a sexual relationship, he thought I was too special to ruin what God had given him. What he desired was uncompromising, unquenchable love. Not just husband and wife love, but the kind of love only God could give a relationship. I believe Jeff fell in love with the Lynnette God restored. This is what drew him to me.

Within the first three months of our relationship, Jeff did something incredible which made him different and yes, worthy of my love. Jeff sat me down on his lap. He asked me to show him all of my bills and how much income I was bringing in. Now, under normal circumstances, this man wouldn't have gotten a glimpse of any financial data on me. But again, this was different. Reluctantly, I showed him my paycheck stub and how much I was paying out. He said so lovingly, "Lynnette, God told me to take care of you, because of that, I can see the van is your biggest financial burden which seems to be eating up most of your money. What is the name of your lender?" I gave him the name and address, but I really didn't believe he could do anything more than talk to the agency to get the payment a little lower. Two days later I received a phone call from the lender asking me to whom and where they should send the title to the car. He paid over nine thousand dollars in cash to pay off my van. His love for me didn't stop there, he took over my bills and paid them all for me. He then put me on an allowance of one hundred and fifty dollars a week for food and gas while he took care of the rest. I wasn't wanting for anything. Every bill was paid on time. The new furniture I just bought a few months earlier was paid off by the love of this man. When he got done, I owed no one. This was truly Boaz. Yes, I questioned and often said, "What if I choose not to marry you, how can I possibly pay you back?" He would always answer in the same way. "I'm not worried about you marrying me, girl. God told me that you were my wife from the day I laid eyes on you."

Breaking Of Old Chains

It wasn't long before we were tested in that love. Like I said before, the angels were rejoicing over our union but the enemy wasn't. Somehow, the young gentleman who abused and harassed me found out about my newfound happiness. All earthly and spiritual hell broke loose when he heard I was getting married. I believe a war broke out in heaven against hell over Jeff and me. As if from out of nowhere, the harassment became almost impossible to deal with.

He followed me to work and church. Everywhere I went, there he was. I would fall asleep, only to be awakened around 2:00 in the morning, to see him in my apartment parking lot, with his truck lights glaring at my front door. He even went as far as finding out Jeff's information. He researched it on the Internet, and then called him to tell him incredible eccentric lies about me.

Because I lived in Delaware, the police would respond in a quicker more concerned fashion. They approached him and warned him not to come near my home or he would be arrested onsite. One night Jeff came into town to see me. We were watching TV when a horrible, crazed pounding interrupted our peaceful time together. The young man began to quote scriptures and screamed out my name saying Jeff was the devil sent to send me to hell. I called the police, but before they could get there, he jumped into his truck and rode off. Within minutes, the sheriff was knocking on the door asking if we were okay. He explained they already had police patrolling the area. The sheriff asked for information about where he could find the young man's home. I gave him his address and phone number and asked what they could do to help stop this nightmare. The sheriff smiled and said "Ma'am, I will go to his house tomorrow and personally inform him of the harassment laws. If he puts up any resistance or comes even to the outskirts of the city I will have him thrown in jail." "Thank you officer," I said and closed the door. I fooled myself in thinking I could somehow still enjoy my evening, however, it wasn't a good ten minutes after the sheriff left that the young man began pounding on my door again. I looked out the window and noticed he had changed his car. He called me every name out of the book, in the book, and from someone else's book. He even tried to tell Jeff I was a whore and a liar and I wasn't worthy of him. I called the police again. Before I could hang up the phone, the young man left. My neighbors told the sheriff everything and explained how this young man has done this on numerous occasions. After hearing everyone's complaint, the sheriff posted an officer on the apartment grounds. Fear came in me, not of the young man, but of losing Jeff. My mind began to play tricks on me. Worry and anxiety came into my soul like a huge wave at sea. What if Jeff decides the hassle isn't worth it? I wonder if he believes the young man? This young man has tried to intimidate everyone who has cared or tried to love me. From my family, to the only man who ever cared enough to see the real me. I kept looking at Jeff trying to read his expressions. I wanted to see if I lost any ground with him. Jeff went into the kitchen, got something to drink, sat back down on the couch, and asked me if I was okay. I knew then he wasn't going anywhere.

"Jeff, I feel as though I owe you an apology for this drama that seems to follow me everywhere I go." I said humbly. "You do not need to apologize," he replied, "This is not your fault. That boy is crazy, and you had nothing to do with that. I am going to stay and make sure he doesn't come back". "Thank you Jeff," I said and wrapped myself in his arms.

We talked about the situation and I told him the long story about all I have gone through with this young man. "I just don't understand how it can continue. He never wanted me or loved me. All he wanted was control over me." I began to cry for this was the first time anyone listened to me and didn't blame me for what had happened. "Lynnette, I will never leave you, I love you." Jeff reached out and held me. What security it was. We talked all night long. My heart was opened and he saw the pain, the hurt and the healing. He understood what he would be getting when he married me. No secrets. No surprises.

The next day we all went to church together at New Covenant. It was so wonderful to walk into the church with the man who loved me more than I loved myself. As usual, church was awesome. We had planned to go out to dinner with the children and then Jeff was going to go back to Canton, Ohio. Jeff, the children and I were walking out of the church when I heard this awful spurting out of my name. Never before have I heard my name said with such revulsion and vileness. "Lynnette". I turned to see who would say my name in such a way. There he was, the young man standing in the parlor of my church, getting louder with every passing second. Jeff turned to the young man, looked him in the eye and asked, "What do you want?" Jeff wasn't nice about anything. The veins in his neck began to protrude and his muscles started to flex. Again Jeff asked, "What do you want and why do you keep harassing Lynnette?" For the first time the young man took a step back. His eyes lost their piercing focus and there was fear. "I'm going to ask you one more time son, what do you want?" Jeff said with his teeth gritted together. The young man knew he had met his match. Jeff dealt with the spirit and not the man. "What are your intentions with her?" The young man asked. It was so obvious he couldn't come up with anything else. "That is absolutely none of your concern. But since you want to know, she will be my wife." The young man almost choked when he replied, "Sir, I see that you are an educated man. Do you really think you can take care of her and the children? You see sir, I love her too." Jeff looked deep in the young man's eyes and said, "You will leave her and her children alone or you will deal with me, do I make myself clear?" The young man took a couple of steps back. Jeff looked at me and said, "Take the children and head towards the car, Lynnette." I quickly gathered the children around me and lead them to the car. Jeff followed as he took one last look at the young man as if to give him one more warning. I turned to see where Jeff was. At that moment, I saw the eyes of the young man. Hatred, wickedness and corruption spilled out of his pores. As we were walking away, he screamed like what sounded like a demonic roar, "Everyone is going to know who you are Lynnette. You are nothing, you hear me, nothing!" Jeff grabbed hold of my hand and escorted me slowly, but with confidence to the car. As we drove off, the men of the church came out and began to say things to the young man. Somehow I knew I was free. Free of the torment, free from the torture and free from the harassment. From that day on, I have never seenor heard from him again.

    Jeff had a face-off with the very demon that was trying to keep me in bondage and ripped me out of his teeth. His love broke the chains forever. I looked out the window as we were driving away. Tears rolled down my cheeks as I began to realize what God had done for me. "Lord," I whispered "You loved me so much that You sent representation of your love here to set me free. Once again you saved me. Not just on Calvary, but today, this very day, You set me free again. I thank You Lord for Your gift of love. I praise You Lord for Your touch and protection. As the lion of torment roared, You the Lion of Judah won. Thank you."

Here is one important fact God revealed to me. Satan had assigned the young man to keep me from ever knowing who I was and from ever knowing Jeff. The torment and cruelty of this young man lasted on and off for seven long years. What Satan didn't realize was God already preordained my redemption. There was absolutely nothing Satan could do to keep me from my destiny. That is why he fought me so hard. As long as I didn't know who I was, Satan had the power. But as soon as God revealed Himself to me, I was free.

The Wedding Gift

Jeff and I began looking at houses. I was actually looking at houses. Now, this may not mean too much to some of you but for a girl who was once on welfare, everything God showed me or gave me a glance of brought me extreme joy. We went into the nice areas too. The first house had water in the basement. Even though it was very nice and located in the Avondale Area, I couldn't see myself looking for a boat to paddle up the stairs everyday. The next house we looked at was perfect. The yard itself was a football field long. It had a basketball court for Shaila and a tree house already in place. The front of the yard reminded me of my grandparent's house. Jeff and I called our realtor right away to view the inside. It was truly lovely. The girls had enough closet space and Joshua had his very own room. The basement had enough area for Jeffery's workout equipment and my kitchen was wonderful. We placed a bid on the house, signed all the necessary paperwork and waited. We were told it would take thirty days to close on the house. Jeff became concerned, but after seeing and experiencing how my God worked, I boldly informed Jeff the house would be ours in two weeks. I went back to Columbus and began to pack up the apartment. Exactly two weeks went by when Jeff called and said, "Honey you will not believe this, but I have the keys to the house. It is ours." I rejoiced and began to praise the Lord for His loyal kindness to Jeff and me. We made an offer on the home on September 14, 1999. The date we received the keys to the house was September 30, 1999. When Jeff handed me my keys, he said to me, "Honey, this is your wedding present. Welcome home." Tears rolled down my cheeks because his words were so true. Everything that was robbed from me by my past mistakes or the mistakes of others, God Himself restored. This was just the beginning.

The Wedding Day

I really don't have to tell you about wedding days. Some are hectic and some are calm. Our wedding started out being a little bit of both. The day was Saturday October 30, 1999. Normally around this time the weather begins to get colder and fall starts its full impact of glory. For some reason, I truly believe because of our wedding, the angels saw fit to begin preparations for our big day.

It wasn't so long ago, when my soon to be husband had been in a lot of pain. He was married before and his ex-wife hurt him deeply. He told me of the long nights of tears and how there were days in which he thought his soul would evaporate into the darkness. He even shared with me of how he lost a part of himself when

A Kept Woman

she left. On Christmas day of 1998, he was curled up in a ball on his couch lying in the dark, crying and depressed over his life. This very place of darkness is where Jesus met him. He gave all of his loneliness and pain over to Christ and left it with Him. When he finally got off the couch, he was a new man. A man who knew exactly who he was and who God was in him. This was his time of preparation for me. "Honey", he said, "I can't even remember the pain I felt. I know it happened, but it was a moment that carries no scars or weight in my life". The opening of my man's most intimate thoughts and memories only made me love him more. So you see when I say that the angels were rejoicing and getting ready for my wedding, I know what I am talking about.

Let me tell you about how excited God was about Jeff and me. The day started off being 72 degrees. The sun shown from the moment we woke till around 8:00 pm that evening. There were no clouds in the sky and the birds were chirping the wedding song.

Because of our past marriages, Jeff and I only invited the people we knew would support us. We did not want anyone there who would hinder or curse our union. We carefully selected thirty people and only fifteen of them came to the wedding. It didn't matter because the angels filled the benches. Rays of sunshine shown through the windows of the church and rested upon the benches.

Jeffery and the men who stood with him, looked incredible at the front of the altar. The song entitled *The Lady, Her Lover and Her Lord* was playing in the background as the men walked to their post. The children, who by the way were also getting married, began their march up the aisle. First Garra, then Shaila and then Joshua, danced as they approached their destination. Then, it was my turn. To another song from the *TD Jakes Love Ballads* called *When God Gave Me You*, I began to walk down the aisle. I set my eyes towards my destiny. Jeffery smiled as I entered the room. I saw my future mother-in-law with tears in her eyes. My aunts smiled with relief and joy as I came towards my new life. Jeff walked up to me and put his arm in perfect synchronization with mine. We turned and faced Pastor Fowler joined as one. As the ceremony went on, Jeffery placed his ring on my finger and then went to Garra and repeated the same vows and placed a ring on her finger. He then went to Shaila and Joshua and repeated the process. We were now all joined as a union. No one was left out. Whatever discord was sown in the beginning of my life was now fully destroyed. I was loved by my husband and my God. "I now pronounce you man and wife and I present to the audience Mr. and Mrs. Jeffery L. Appling". This was music to my ears, my soul and my heart. If I listened carefully, I could hear the angels singing and clapping. They rejoiced for me because God married me and then allowed me to experience His love through another individual. All I could think about was the scripture, *This is the Lord's doing, it is marvelous in our eyes. This is the day that the Lord thy God has made, and I shall rejoice and be glad in it. Psalms 118:23-24* KJV

The Garden

It wasn't long after we were happily married, that my husband adopted my children. It was at this point in my life when God showed me just a small part of the covenant He made with me. I have already explained the children's biological father had nothing to do with them. I saw the pain growing inside my son and the longing he had of knowing just who he was. You see, I could identify this spirit because I carried it for so long. Shaila was acting out her anger by breaking things in the house and hiding the broken items in the basement. This in itself symbolized the brokenness she felt inside. The hiding of items in the basement expressed her deepest psyche. Hiding is the easiest route to take which leads to loneliness and the feeling of abandonment. To hide things deep in the only place no one would ever dare to look... within, becomes a dark basement filled with cobwebs of the past overflowing with things we may forget are there, but nevertheless, are still there. Destroying dishes was a temporary fix that added a smile to her face for the moment. I knew of this pain well. For many years my basement was filled with broken things. Garra, of course, was too young to care or know what she was missing. Seeing all of this played out brought my husband and I to the conclusion that our children needed closure.

I was never a mother who told my kids not to love their biological father. As a matter of fact, I encouraged their love for him with balance. In spite of that, my children were secretly hurting inside. I never wanted them to experience any of the pain I felt as a child, or to believe they were alone. I took my experiences and started to minister to my children. This was significant to me, for how could I minister to the world in whatever capacity God had for me and not love, understand and serve my family?

I prayed for guidance on how to deliver my children and for God to teach me on how to minister to them. I asked Him for wisdom and knowledge as well as mercy, compassion and grace. These were the key ingredients to loving my children past their pain. It was my responsibility to teach them who they are and to instill in them the skills on how to seek the face of God. I gave my children back to the Lord for His service to do whatever He deemed necessary. This is the first revelation of wisdom... to understand my children did not belong to me as a piece of property, but were entrusted into my care for a higher purpose. They were my garden. I was to grow them up to be the fruit they needed to be. If God called them to be an apple, then they better look like an apple, taste like an apple and bake like an apple. They were not to be a strange fruit on someone else's tree or in another garden.

God presented it to me in a very clear and precise way. When He desires to use my fruit and plucks from any one of my three trees, Shaila, Joshua or Garra, in my garden, He expects growth, nourishment and seed. The apple must be able to be eaten to serve not only God, but if He chooses to bake an apple pie, it must be ripe enough to feed a multitude. This apple must be ready to do service in the Kingdom. He then showed me how He takes a bite out of the apple to see and examine the seed. If there is no seed, how can He plant and reproduce this tree? What is the seed? It is the Word of God. My trees will not flourish without future seed to invest. This Word must be embedded deep into the hearts of my children in order for them to know who they are and where they are going.

Because of this, each day I began to examine myself and the role I hold as a parent and steward. I realized being a parent is more than just putting a roof over my children's head. It is being a spiritual covering. Jeff and I were my children's gatekeepers. Nothing was to enter that was not of God and nothing was to leave that was planted by God.

My first step was to understand the calling on each one of their lives. God revealed to me who they were by the names that were placed upon them. The Holy Spirit explained the name of **Shaila Ly-Nette Appling** to me. Shaila is the East Indies name for the Mt. Sinai Mountain. This literally means *The place where God rests*. Ly-Nette is French for *beautiful* and Appling means, *to reproduce after its own kind or one who continuously carries seed*. Shaila is destined to carry the anointing of God, to stand flat-footed on His Word, to be a beautiful sweet aroma to Him, to speak His Word and bring about change in ones life. This brings seed to be used for the Kingdom of God. The name **Joshua Forte' Appling** was clarified also. Joshua means *strong leader of God or one who leads*. *Forte' is a *hilt of a sword, the part between the handle and the blade*. In addition it means *loud or strong and Appling means *to reproduce after it's own kind or one who continuously carries seed*. Joshua Forte' Appling's destiny is to be a strong leader of God who speaks His Word and proclaims the Word of God. He is to help bring about change in ones life. And last but not least, **Garra Lyne' Appling's** meaning was told to me by the Holy Spirit. Garra is the Hebrew word for *grain or seed*. In botanical usage, grain is not a seed, but a fruit. Lyne' means *beautiful* and Appling means *to reproduce after it's own kind or one who continuously carries seed*. So, Garra Lyne' Appling's destiny is to be a fruit or seed which is so beautiful and nourishing it draws others to Christ. She can be used in any way deemed necessary by God. Be it as a seed who will reproduce other seed or a fruit used to feed others. Either way she is blessed and loved by God.

A Kept Woman

In response to this research, I stopped speaking over our children what man saw, and began to show them and speak over them what God called them to be. This action started the breaking of the curse. What curse? Because of the life I had before, my baggage and issues flowed to my children. They were all carriers just like their mother. I refuse to let Satan destroy, mimic or deny my children their natural and spiritual rights to have access to the Kingdom of God. Jeff and I took charge over the situation and began a process of life.

God also revealed to me that because my ex-husband denied his own destiny in his children, they would be given to another to carry on their new father's legacy. Let me help you to understand. By any man or woman denying their very own children cancels out your blessing of human seed. What do I mean? Children are the most precious gift God can give a person. They carry your name, your heart, and your bloodline to the very next generation. When my husband adopted my children, he planted his seed within my children and called them his. This act cannot be reversed. By law an adopted father cannot abandon his children. Now, the harvest of that seed is his. There will not be an acknowledgement by God or mankind that will allow my ex-husband to have access or a claim to the new harvest. Grandchildren, and their children and so on, now carry the bloodline spiritually and, yes naturally of Jeffery Appling. When men look at the birth certificate, it says Jeffery L. Appling as the father. My ex-husband has given up and lost forever his namesake and his seed of long life.

The second thing God had me understand was my children's name was their destiny but the call in their life was their purpose. Shaila is called to be an Evangelist, Joshua is a Preacher/Pastor, and Garra is the Praise and Worshipper. It was now my responsibility to make sure they continue to walk towards their purpose.

After much prayer and fasting and hearing directly from the Lord, I began my parental duty to train them up in the way they should go. This means that I raise my children according to the mindset of God. I stopped apologizing for my beliefs and enforced the truth in my children's life. I believe the highest calling I have is to be a good steward over God's property. My children each were saved and filled with the Holy Spirit. They manifest the presence of the Lord in their lives. They have been called peculiar and strange. Therefore they will never fit into anyone else's garden but their own.

My family and I started to have Bible Study on Thursday nights. During this time we read together and answer any questions they may have in regards to the Word of God. Jeff and I taught our children how to stand flatfooted on the Word of God without wavering in their beliefs, yet at the same time to have compassion and mercy. We showed them through our own relationship and by the cherished and valued treatment of one another of how love is manifested, what love is all about and how they never have to be authenticated by man. This process of teaching continues on even today.

When I look at my children, I realize they will be more powerful than I could ever imagine. They have the advantage of having both Jeff and I in their lives to guide them and protect them. They will start where Jeff and I end. It took me thirty-three years to understand my calling and another five years to begin to walk in it. My children are still young and already know who they are in Christ and what their purpose is in the Kingdom. It is Jeff and my duty and highest service to prepare them for the war against Satan. When they go into battle and they will, they will understand and know how to strategically destroy his hold over others and the world. His tactics will not deceive them and they will come forth victorious. This is the inheritance of those who are called by God. I claim my children for the Kingdom of God and will have them live by Isaiah 54.

And all thy children shall be taught of Jehovah; and great shall be the peace of thy children. In righteousness shall thou be established: thou shall be far from oppression, for thou shall not fear; and from terror, for it shall not come near thee. No weapon that is formed against thee shall prosper; and every tongue that shall rise against thee in judgment thou shall condemn. This is the heritage of the servants of Jehovah, and their righteousness, which is of me, saith Jehovah. (Isaiah 54:14-17)

A Kept Woman

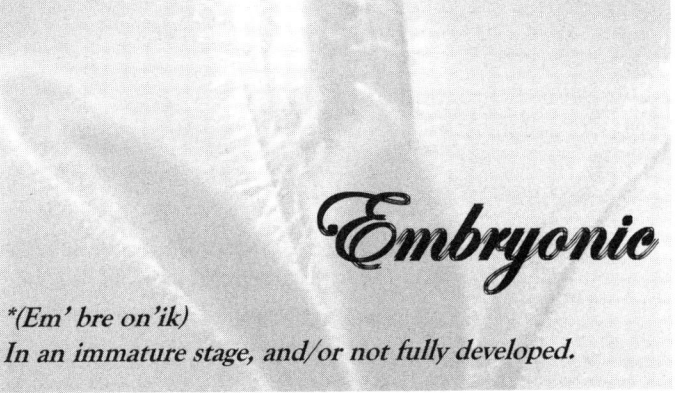

Embryonic

(Em' bre on'ik)
In an immature stage, and/or not fully developed.

Lynnette Tiller Appling

Treasure Hunting

After finally getting settled and understanding my purpose with my new husband and children, now it was time to find out more about what God desired from me. It was now time to go on a treasure hunt. Somewhere deep inside me God established gifts and purpose and I was going to dig it out, open up the trunk and find out the true value and worth of these treasures. I was bold enough to believe there was more than one treasure chest crammed with exciting and prominent stuff. I was determined to find them all, no matter how deep down I had to go.

I started with a map. Not just any map, but the one God showed me on the ceiling not too long ago. Looking back I saw how the path I was once on took a sudden turn. It was at this turn the treasure hunt would begin.

In following the road which led to my victory, I was able to see how every single incident in my life led me to this moment in time. From the first marriage to Chute Gerdeman, the people in my life were strategically placed to push me into my destiny. Each job trained me for the next job and those jobs prepared me for what would soon be my greatest job of all. Every coincidence, every deceitful thing done to destroy me, every wonderful moment was all done to lead me to the face of Christ. The Holy Spirit guided my mind to the truth. I was not just some child born by mistake or because two people got together. I was ordained to be here. The question is why? I understood the road and the turns, but I desired to have complete knowledge of the *why*. Why did God spare me? Why didn't I die? Why was He always with me? Why did He choose me? And what were the treasures and their purpose?

Seeing His Eyes

Exodus 33:20 BEB – But it is not possible for you to see my face, for no man may see Me and still go on living.

I began to ask God my questions of *why*, not out of disrespect or lack of reverence, but out of wanting knowledge and desiring wisdom. I searched the Word and came across Moses and his request to see the glory of God. So I asked God the same question as Moses. I said, "Lord, allow me to see Your glory. For I desire to see You in the most intimate way. Not for my glory or of any vanity of my own, but out of just simply wanting You. I want to know You as my God, my friend, and my lover. I don't want a superficial relationship with You. I ask for this intimacy in order to know Your heart, Your thoughts, and Your desires. May I, Father, see my Daddy's face?" I waited to hear His reply and began to speak from my heart again. "Daddy, nothing about my old self wants to live. I don't want to go back to the self-centered, hurt Lynnette, and in order to do this I must be in You and You in me. With this transformation of me being molded into Your character, Your love, Your image, even Your structure, I need to see Your eyes. Allow me to see Your eyes Daddy. Permit Lynnette's mindset and ways of thinking and living to die, so that Your mindset and ways may live in me." Suddenly, I heard laughter from the heavens. I knew I pleased my Daddy by this request. In the middle of my living room, the ceiling began to turn. I fell to my knees in honor of the Almighty King, yet kept my eyes on the ceiling. It spun until I could see the outdoors. God spoke to me and said, "What you bind on earth shall be bound in heaven and what you bless on earth shall be blessed in heaven. When you pray, it will open the gates of hell and hell must release everything Satan has stolen. Because you have asked for Me, I give you the keys to both heaven and hell." I laid and cried until I was weak in my own flesh. The ceiling closed up and there was silence. I dared not move but lay prostrate in the Presence of the Lord.

Slowly, I trembled getting up and sat quietly and humbly on my couch. I was speechless once again. I didn't move from that spot for over an hour. My mind could not grasp what had just happened. I knew I received a blessing from my Father in heaven, but still didn't know the depths of the blessing He just bestowed upon me.

This request to know Him in a more intimate way was not based on the law of the Old Testament. I took this verse and applied the revelation of Romans 8:13- *For if ye **live** after the* *flesh, ye shall die: but if ye through the Spirit do mortify the deeds of the body, ye shall **live**.* Did I see His face you ask? Yes. He has never let go of my face. He keeps me focused on Him and Him alone. Every time I have a thought, which is not pure, or I am about to make a mistake, He pulls my face towards His eyes, and my motives die. I never want to be out of His presence or away from His face. Do I see His face? Daily. As I am continuously being molded into His image and becoming more like my Daddy Jesus, I can look in the mirror and see Him.

From Within Psalms of Lament

The days became full with anticipation of what God would do. I would wake in the morning, pour two cups of coffee, one for me, one for Jesus, pull out my Bible and start to read. "What will we be discussing today?" I would ask the Lord. I literally imagined Him coming and sitting at the dinning room table with slippers and a robe on, just like me, and sipping His coffee while we discussed His heart. I would never remove His cup until the end of the day when I would prepare for the next morning.

One evening after an intimate day with Jesus, Jeff came home from work. He had this habit of always drinking what was left out that he thought was mine. I saw him eyeballing the cup of cold coffee which was left on the dinning room table. "You don't want to drink that Jeff. It belongs to Jesus", I said. Jeff replied "I am sure He wouldn't mind me drinking a cold cup of coffee since He left it here". Without a second thought Jeff drank the coffee straight down. "Jeff" I said, "That was a bad move". He chuckled in disbelief of my story of how Jesus and I met every morning for a chat.

That night Jeff tried to sleep but was awake all night. Well this seems normal you are probably saying. And for most people who don't drink coffee on a regular basis, I would agree. However, Jeff was up for over seventy-two hours because of his lack of respect for Jesus' cup of coffee. After this, he believed me when I said, "Jesus stopped by today".

Because of the intimacy God and I were having, He gave me music from heaven to write. Though I had a few songs from the year before, He prompted me to continue writing and preparing. One morning I was looking outside the window into my yard. I was impressed with the movement by the majestic trees. I watched the squirrels run freely and heard the birds chirping a harmonic sound which seemed to be carried to the uttermost parts of the world by the blowing of the wind. I thought to myself, "Behold, the awesome love of God". I felt safe and secure in this new arena of life. I quickly picked up a pencil and began to hum a melody to the words. I wrote:

> *The awesome love of God*
> *Surrounds my heart and makes me sing*
> *The mercy of His forgiving blood*
> *Gives my soul wings*
> *The glory of His wondrous throne*
> *Make me know I'm not alone*
> *The beauty of His healing word*
> *Gives my spirit hope*
> *How can I not know He's real?*
> *When my life can easily reveal*
> *I can look around and see*
> *His mercy all around me*
> *When I look around and see*
> *What my God has done for me*
> *My soul cries out because it's free*
> *My song begins to sing*
> *My song begins to sing...Amen.*

This song evolved and was the catalyst for the CD *From Within Psalms of Lament*. This CD told the story of my life and how God brought me out of my land of Egypt into my promised land of Canaan. I studied the Psalms and learned as much as I could about David and his worship. I desired the same type of relationship David had with God through worship. Worship in itself is a place that cannot in human words be described. It is a place so intimate, so life changing, so precious. We must be very careful to always cherish this access to God's throne. I personally value this key more than any other. I knew His love transposed His grace and mercy to me when I thought there was none and for this I am grateful.

As I moved towards the progression of the CD there were still those voices from the past that continued to tell me I could not do this, I had an inadequate voice, or my voice was not good enough to make a CD. They tried their best to stop me from singing and making the CD. Voices such as an evangelist from Columbus, Ohio who I used to work for who told me the only skill I had was answering a phone. There were people who said the only reason I was making a CD was to try to compete or keep up with my sister Mary, who was already very successful in a gospel group and had won numerous awards with them.

The problem was no one tried to know my heart. No one knew my story. Still, they were doing their best to write the story for me. I am not going to tell you I was so holy that the words of these particular people did not penetrate my spirit. On the contrary. They did intimidate me and were a stronghold in my life. I concerned myself with how others viewed me or received from me. I knew my past. I knew what I had been through. This was the very thing Satan used to try to keep me from fulfilling the musical rendition of God's faithfulness. I almost failed this test until I remembered how every time I couldn't make it, none of them were there. I remembered the intimate time and special moments I had with God. This love we have far outweighed their opinions or their thoughts. Because of this the title of the CD became apparent. *From Within, Psalms of Lament.* This CD added to my very being. In writing, and singing about God's love, I was able to break some old stuff that occupied a strong seat in the front row of my life. When I lamented before the Lord, He always heard me. My lamenting did not stay at a place of wonderment but brought me to a place of praise and worship immediately taking my eyes off of me, and directing them right back to Christ.

The CD recording took on a more justified persona, because now I could sing from experience. I could look at my husband in the studio and sing from the depths of my soul.

Being the covering that he was, my husband Jeffery paid for the entire process of recording. He believed so much this CD was from God. He invested his seed into it. When the CD was complete, the cost of it came to twenty-two thousand dollars. This is not said to brag, but to give God the complete glory. Let me explain. God has taught me to always seed into good ground. So many times we seed into other people's dreams or visions, which is ordained by God to do. But God taught Jeff and I to seed into ourselves also, for we too are good ground. This money was seed money. I was unknown and had never produced a recording. God gave us the knowledge and the know how to get the job done. Because of this type of faith and seed, hundreds have been blessed and delivered. We are not looking for money as the reward, but we desire to harvest the souls.

After the CD was finished, God placed a very special radio station in my life which continues to this day to support the ministry in which God continues to pour out of my belly. This station is WINW Joy 1520 AM under the direction of Curtis Perry III. He played the songs *I Can't Give Up, Hold On* and *The Awesome Love Of God*. These songs became immediate hits. Other radio stations throughout Ohio followed suit and the CD was on its way, ministering a word of love from the heart of God to the people.

Once the CD was released, Jeff and I decided to have a CD Premiere in Columbus, Ohio at the Hyatt Regency. This premiere was only ten days before our first anniversary so we thought we would have the premiere and then go away to celebrate our first year of marriage. Little did I know this moment in time would thrust us into the right position for the purpose of our lives.

The Birthing Process

1. The act of coming into life; fact of being born
2. Beginning or origin
3. A bringing forth

Lynnette Tiller Appling

Defining The Purpose

The premiere went extremely well. People I had not seen in the last year were there to support the official release of the CD and the Awesome Love of God video. Other people who were a strong force in my life during the time I was in Columbus, Ohio also attended to show their support. It was a wonderful moment in time because this was my first real opportunity to open up about the CD and my past. Still, I held back all the things I was feeling at the moment because I felt in my spirit it was not the right time to open my heart. God was still developing me. I was still healing. I came to realize healing takes time and it is truly a process. It can't be rushed. I've also learned that deep healing is never ending. Once you think you're over one thing God surfaces something else to deal with. He is so merciful to not have us deal with all our junk at one time. We would be an emotional and spiritual wreck if we did.

Looking over the audience, I saw some people who placed themselves in a position of enemies and some who sat as seasonal friends, as well as those precious few who positioned themselves in the place of lifetime friends. My heart grew bigger and a little restrained. Me, restrained, seems impossible, but it was true. This restraint was done only by understanding the process of forgiveness. They each had a significant role and duty to carry out in my life so I might come to a position of kneeling at the Lord's feet. Something was beginning to stir in my soul. I sensed something was changing. I could feel the course of my life turning in the wind. Purpose was being birthed.

After the premiere, Jeff and I went away to an intimate resort. I enjoyed my anniversary with my husband. Not only because it was our first year anniversary, but because there was rest. We played a mean and competitive game of pool. Jeff will deny to this day the fact that he was about to be beat. We walked, we dined, we talked, we cuddled and we loved. In the midst of all of this I felt something pulling at me.

On Saturday morning, I asked my husband to stop by a drug store to get me a notebook. In this inexpensive half-size notebook is where I wrote my most intimate feelings. I felt in my spirit an urgency to spend quiet time meditating and enjoying the moment. I could tell moments like this would be few and far between. I could discern the time and the season was changing. God wanted me to rest on this vacation for the season of seeding had begun.

I sat by the whirlpool and began to write. What I wrote in the journal helped birth my purpose. As I was writing the Holy Ghost took over and prophesied to my spirit. At that time the music I wrote would only be a vehicle used to get me in the door of people's hearts. I must speak and prophesy the Word of God. My purpose was to bring a message of complete healing. I didn't know how this was going to happen, but it was clear this was the road this ministry was taking. As I finished writing my first insert, I looked at the water to reflect. I was nervous and excited. I had conceived in my spirit and from that moment on was carrying a new life.

L.T.A. Productions

During our dating stage, Jeff and I created a company called L.T.A. Productions. Originally, it meant Lynnette Tiller and Appling Productions, but God molded it to simply be L.T.A. Productions meaning Love, Truth and Anointing. L.T.A. became a vehicle used to produce some of the most amazing concerts in the city of Canton as well as the state of Ohio. The anointing flowed as God expanded the ministry from just Jeff and me to a group of forty people. The joy and love which came from creating the From Within CD connected Jeff and me to some wonderful people.

We traveled the state singing and speaking in a concert format. The anointing of God moved with us and was life changing. We saw people from all walks of life being touched, healed and delivered. For the first year, booking engagements were weekly. The Holy Spirit was governing us on which engagements to take. There were some engagements where there was only one person. But that didn't detour me. I pulled

A Kept Woman

up a chair and ministered to that one person.

I remember one particular engagement in Wooster, Ohio in which I was to give a concert at one of the bookstores in town. I was aching in my body and didn't feel quite right. I had a sore throat and was sucking on throat lozenges, but I was determined to be obedient to the Holy Spirit. I looked around the store and there was not one person other than the management there. The management didn't seem too interested in what we were doing. I looked at Jeff and said, "This is definitely to the Glory of God, for only He will hear this song". I opened with If I Could Just Touch You and started to give my testimony of His divine intervention. I went to the next song, and the next song and suddenly the Holy Spirit said, "This is your last song". I looked at Jeff and told him what the spirit of the Lord had spoken. I ended with I Give My Life, said goodnight as if there were a crowd of people there and closed up shop. Jeffery didn't agree with my decision and became a little irritated. We went out to dinner and I began to explain to him what God had done.

"Honey", I said, "I was being tested tonight on whether I would sing and speak in season as well as out of season. Because I was obedient, God will bless the seed that has been sown. Even if I don't reap it, He will." Jeffery understood. We both learned to be obedient through the small beginnings.

We didn't make a lot of money, but again, it wasn't about money. I was truly not looking for fame or glory, but my heart was going out for the women. Every time I sang, I was singing to the women. I saw their pain and discerned their lack of understanding. I knew their story. I just wrote it. Nothing they could say would shock me or change what I felt towards them. The anointing was piercing and strong. Whenever we ministered to the women, prophecy always came.

Women followed me to my car and asked for prayer. Teenage girls began to call me mom. My spiritual eyes were opened to their situation. I understood the mandate on my life to declare war on Satan. Satan had to let these women go. I desired truth for them. My heart began to be burdened with their issues. Sometimes I wanted to shake the women and wake them up.

Their problems were heavy on me. I was an intercessor and didn't know how to let go of the burden and leave it at Jesus' feet. I grew tired and wanted to step out of the spiritual arena for a while. My heart was heavy and I felt loaded down.

Jeff and I were in the bedroom when I told him of my feelings. I looked at him and said, "You know Jeff, no-one has ever said I am the apple of their eye. I know this isn't important, but just once, I would like to hear it." I chuckled to keep it from being too serious of a conversation and to make sure Jeff knew this was no reflection on him. I prayed for guidance and deliverance myself. Because I didn't have an overseer at this time who was capable of understanding the call on my life, I had no direction.

I ran into a mind-set roadblock in Canton, Ohio. If you didn't do things the way they always been done, then you were a troublemaker. If you made the people think outside the box, then of course you were practicing witchcraft. Let's call it like it is, a religious spirit, jealousy and insecurity. Pastors were afraid that you just might take a member out of his or her church. Not realizing that as pastors, they are to equip people to be ambassadors for Christ, meaning to go out, represent and tell the good news that mankind can be delivered.

Understanding The True Vision

During this time of spiritual growth and change, I decided to end the summer with one last concert. I sought the Holy Spirit to find a theme for it. I wanted an intimate evening which could be used as an avenue for the women to share what they were feeling. I called it Ladies Night Out In the Presence of God Assembly.

I called a couple of churches to see if I could have this event at their facility. Finally after several attempts, one of them accepted. The band started to prepare for this event. We advertised, ran promotions and really put it out there to the city.

At last, the night came. I initiated prayer. I knew my spirit was tired. "Lord, meet me here tonight" I said. "I need Your breath to stimulate my soul". I watched as the opening ministers began their numbers and looked into the audience. There was only a handful of women in attendance. This is when my flesh began to rise. "That's it, I'm done," I thought. "Why continue to pour into these people who keep looking at the dead dried up well wondering when the water is going rise to the top. I just can't do it anymore. It is too hard," I said under my breath. I was always careful not to have anyone not believe God was with me due to my actions or words.

I walked out to the stage to sing. The weight I was carrying began to lift off of me. Even though I was discouraged, God began to minister to me. Here I thought I was giving something to the women and God used this opportunity to fill me up. With my eyes shut and my head bowed, I sang to myself. This had never happened before. The words of the songs I had written out of my pain were the very tools used to nourish my spirit.

As I ended the concert I walked to the back of the building and began to praise God for being with me once again. The dread of singing or speaking was gone and I was refreshed in my body and spirit. As I turned from praising Him, one of my assistants came to me and told me there were some women wanting to speak to me. Pulling myself together, I closed my eyes and said a prayer in my heart. "Lord if this is the road that you wish for me to travel, then I will go." I opened my heart and mind to the opportunities He had destined for me.

I walked with my assistant to the group of women. Immediately, they encamped me. I became concerned because I was unfamiliar with what was going on. An older lady began to speak in tongues as she grabbed me and drew me to her chest. Praying out of fear, I desired understanding and clarity. "Lord" I whispered, "If this is You, allow me to hear You clearly, identify Yourself to me". My bodyguard tried to break the older woman's grip from me. As he went to touch her arm, a volt of intense heat came through him and shot up his arm. He pulled his hand quickly away and stepped back. Just then I opened my eyes. A voice so clearly was interpreting what the woman was saying. "It is Me, Lynnette. I am pleased with you. I love you Lynnette and you are the apple of My eye." I wept and shook uncontrollably. The woman continued to speak in tongues, when another woman, walked up and said "Lynnette, God said to tell you, you are the apple of His eye." One by one, four more women began to prophecy. One of the woman said, "God is saying, your mission has just begun. Eyes have not seen the destiny He has for you." Prophecy came from each woman. There were about nine women all together. Later I found out they all were evangelists in the community. When God was done, I almost collapsed from the glory of His appearance. There would be a new road I was to travel. The assurance was I was not going to be walking this road alone. That night was a very special night. Here I was thinking I was ministering to the women but God did a reverse on me. He met me when I needed to know what to do.

Ladies Night Out, Inc.

The date is January 1, 2001. Jeff and I just settled in to watch Trinity Broadcast Network and see the New Year programs. After a long year of concerts and traveling, it was nice to cuddle up on the couch with my gorgeous, wonderful, comfortable, intelligent, loving husband. Sorry, I got a little carried away thinking about my man. I was just about to lay my head on his chest and close my eyes, when the voice of the Lord spoke. I have noticed it is when I am not thinking or when I am resting that He shows up the most.

"Lynnette," He said. "Yes, Lord" I spoke out loud. Jeff turned off the TV to listen also. He too heard His voice. "You and Jeff are to begin to have assemblies where the woman of Canton, Ohio can attend and learn about Me." "But, Lord" I asked, "We have never done this before, and how would we do it?" God replied "I have already given you everything you need and have prepared the hearts of servants to help you". "Lord," I asked "How would Jeff and I pay for this and where we would we have it and..." The Lord replied, "I will supply all your needs". Jeff and I looked at each other in silence. "Well, there is no time like the present to get started". I said to Jeff.

I called the people who have been with Jeff and me through the years of traveling. The Lord showed me details of how the ministry should be governed. God instructed me on the directors and their responsibilities. He showed us how to book the speakers and gave me intimate information on what He desired.

He directed my steps to places to meet people and gave me discernment on their gifts. Most of the people He led me to talk to had been through a lot and desired to share their gifts and testimony with other people. God taught me about budgets, contracts, grant writing, 501c.3 implementation, motivating and uplifting the people. He showed me how to set up ministries inside the ministry and guided me on the spirit of excellence. During this process, God began to shape Jeff and I into leaders with qualities to reproduce leadership in others. He wanted the people empowered. Through this, He sanctioned and taught us who we were in the Kingdom. Ladies Night Out, Inc. was born.

Jeff and I started to look for speakers who could bring a healing and deliverance word to Canton, Ohio. One Sunday morning, I was watching Black Entertainment TV and saw a magnificent speaker who was real. What I mean by real is she taught the Word in a way that women could relate to. I said out loud "God, I would love to have her speak at Ladies Night Out, but I know she won't come". The Holy Spirit immediately said back "If you keep canceling out what you want, you're right. No she will not come. But to show you that I am with you, call the number and ask." I stopped braiding my daughter's hair, went downstairs to the computer and typed in her name. I quickly jotted down her information and called the phone number. What transpired was incredible. A wonderful woman said she would be speaking at her conference in November and in order for me to meet her, she would have me come down and speak and sing in West Virginia. The favor of God didn't stop there, she also contacted the speaker's ministry for me and gave a good word for the *Ladies Night Out* ministry. This speaker, who to this day has been a speaker for Ladies Night Out every year, is Pastor Sheryl Brady.

It became a skill to ask the ordained generals to come to the Canton area and minister a word into the atmosphere. The Canton Region was beginning to change and so was I.

On the visit to West Virginia, God had me meet another wonderful prophetess and speaker, Pastor Cheryl Grissom. As I watched her and learned from her, I knew she was to come to Ladies Night Out. She ministered and of course the whole place became a Holy Ghost party. She stepped down out of the pulpit and called me up. "Oh no", I said to myself. You see, no matter where I went to minister, God would seal the prophecy of the nine women. I really thought I had a sign on my head that said, "Call me up."

As I walked toward the front of the church she said to me "Lynnette, do you know who you are?" I replied somewhat confused by the question, "I think I do". I must admit I wasn't too convinced myself. I knew God had His hand on me, but I really didn't know who I was or the office I held. She asked, "Who do people say you are Lynnette?" I again answered in a confused state of where this was leading, but nevertheless, I answered the question. "I have been called Evangelist, Minister, and Psalmist". She asked again "Who did God say that you were?" I closed my eyes and began to search my spirit. I asked the Holy Ghost, "Who am I, and what is the calling on my life?" I opened my eyes and looked at Pastor Grissom. When I opened my mouth out came "I am an Apostle". Astonished at my own response I said to myself "What? You don't even know what that is". Before I could argue with my intellect, she spoke and said, "That is correct." And before I could hear the rest of the prophecy, the Holy Spirit had taken over and I was resting in the cradle of His arms.

The same breath I felt so long ago was now hovering over me and through me. It was like fresh rain in my longing soul. It moistened the very seed God planted in me. I rested in His presence once again as He sealed the truth in my heart.

Another woman who became my spiritual mother (Barbara "Tommi Femrite") confirmed this same prophecy. She never met Pastor Cheryl Grissom until she came to a Ladies Night Out Conference. As she called up my family, she confirmed everything God had said about my children and my husband. When she got to me God made a statement through her and said, "Some say you are a evangelist, some call you minister, others call you psalmist, but I the Lord God call you an Apostle." You guessed it. I was out on the floor again, drunk in the Spirit. God will always confirm His Word and seal it through the confessions of our mouth and others. In the mouth of two or three witnesses shall every word be established (2 Corinthians 13:1 KJV).

After this incredible encounter Jeff and I came home and tried to not have any more engagements until the following year. It was almost the New Year and I wanted to make sure our family enjoyed one another. Jeff and I wanted to take a couple of months to relax. God spoke to me in my dreams. I had dreams of being a warrior and guarding the gateway so the demons could not escape. Other dreams were about me receiving a vessel of oil from my mother and anointing people. Others were of me teaching in Africa. The dreams came almost regularly during this time. All of them carried a message. I kept quiet about them and only told my husband. I knew eventually, God would bring to me someone who would understand them and tell me what they meant.

I called this particular time a year of prophecy. God continued to instill in me His direction and confirmation through many people. Because of this I became sure of my place and embarked on fulfilling His desires of me.

Ladies Night Out International Ministries, formerly Ladies Night Out, Inc., is now traveling around the nation having conferences and assemblies. It has grown to over 102 volunteers. It has established offices in both Northeast Ohio and Southern Ohio. It has brought esteemed speakers and singers to small cities with much deliverance as well as economical upswings for the businesses in the communities.

Ladies Night Out International Ministries has several ministries under its umbrella that endorse empowerment in women and men such as: the Ladies Night Out Empowerment Scholarships for single mothers to go to a school of their choice, Ladies Night Out Debt Release Endowment which helps people who can not pay their bills and teaches them correct management of finances, Girls Night Out which is a mentorship for ages 8-12, Young Ladies Night Out which is a mentorship program for ages 12-18 and provides scholarship funding, Ladies Night Out Operation Give which gives food to the homeless, and Ladies Night Out Missionary Award which awards an outstanding missionary organization or individual who has made a positive impact on the community.

Ladies Night Out also has community fundraisers such as the Ladies Night Out Northeast Ohio Bakeoff, Ladies Night Out Southern Ohio Bakeoff, Ladies Night Out Fall Lasagna Luncheon Fundraiser, Ladies Night Out Benefit Concert and Ladies Night Out Shopping Spree.

In just a few short years, Ladies Night Out International Ministries has become a ministry which has been prophesied as the Pool of Bethesda and has helped to jump start revival in the communities it has blessed.

Quizzes, Tests & Exams

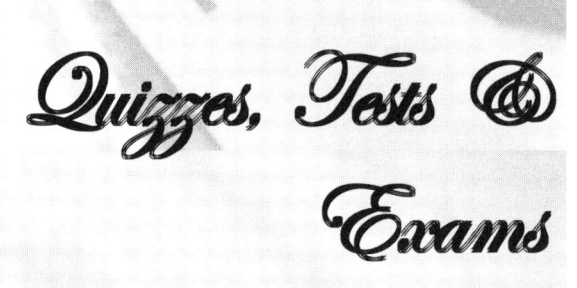

Let it be all joy to you, my brothers, when you undergo tests of every sort, Because you have the knowledge that the testing of your faith gives you the power of going on in hope. But let this power have its full effect, so that you may be made complete, needing nothing...
There is a blessing on the man who undergoes testing because, if he has God's approval, he will be given the crown of life, which the Lord has said He will give to those who have love for Him.
James 1:2-4 and 12 BET

And when all these tests were ended the evil one went away from Him for a time.
Luke 4:13 BET

Lynnette Tiller Appling

Overcoming Hurting People

If 2001 was a year of prophecy then 2002 and 2003 were years of tests, quizzes and exams. The first test I had to pass was the test of overcoming people who were bruised and hurt. This test involves learning how to forgive, to actually release the people from their mistakes and to hold no charge to their account. I am still learning everyday how to let go of unexplained hurt. It is not easy. But allowing God to take the hurt and pain, giving Him complete control is liberating.

There are unfortunate times when a lack of understanding of who we are and the intimate pain of an individual confuses a person's mind. Sometimes unknowingly, we lash out our pain towards other people. This could be people we know intimately or not know at all. Fear of the unknown and fear of having our innermost self exposed paralyzes us into choosing to react in a self-preserving way. No one wants his or her comfort zone shaken. This self-preserving action keeps our wounds from healing because we hold on to what an individual has done. We want to remember the pain because we don't want to give the individual who wounded us an opportunity to hurt us again. This pain becomes the foundation which builds barriers and brick walls. We tend to not trust anyone and can easily settle into the victim syndrome. Now we have an excuse to use at our discretion to keep us from facing the truth or embracing our freedom.

I was this person. I took in and carried everything everyone said as well as took personally the negative behavior towards me and held on to it. Forgiveness, though I knew of it, was not an active part of my lifestyle. I grew exasperated, resentful, frustrated and deeply wounded. Because of these feelings, I wrote a segment before rewriting this one condemning each person and justified my stance in doing so. I really thought I had given my pain over to Christ, but found out only recently the true reason God had me write this section was for my own healing. Now I am praying that what I have learned in the last few months may help you understand the test of character.

Each attack was real. The people who spoke harsh and cruel

words over me are factual. But the truth would not let me give place or position to my pain. The truth is the Word of God. His Word says in Romans 8:37 (KJV) that Nay, in all these things we are more than conquerors through Him that loved us. His Word also says in Malachi 4:2 (KJV) But unto you that fear my name shall the Sun of righteousness arise with healing in His wings; and ye shall go forth, and grow up as calves of the stall. God desired for me to be whole, whole in my thinking, in my being, in my body and my heart. The only way to receive this wholeness was through complete forgiveness. Either I believe and trust in the covering of my Savior or I waver in my faith and doubt His ability to protect my heart.

I didn't want to let go of the pain. I am not talking about the first and second epoch of my life. This kind of pain I could easily see and identify. The type of pain I am expressing is the wound that has a smooth scar over it. It seems and appears to be healed but there is tenderness and inflammation deeply embedded which penetrates within the muscle. Everyone can see something hurt me, yet the outer appearance made it seem as though I was okay.

The common awareness and understanding that allows us to know that all of us go through something is prevalent in everyone's lives. Unfortunately, this common familiarity makes one nonchalant and callous toward someone else's pain. Nevertheless this pain is the type where even the one who has been hurt does not truly grasp or know the depths the weapon used has penetrated. This was me. I was blind to my own inflammation. I grew old in my ways. Settled. It was as if I had arthritis of my spirit. I could still do ministry, still move, but there was so much pain in doing so. Life was a struggle because the unforgiveness in my heart crippled me. My spiritual joints were decaying and I didn't know it.

How could I minister to the very people who were hurting me? It was time for me to learn how to love beyond self. God was preparing and teaching me. He had me study His Word to properly understand His teachings on this very subject.

During this very time of coming to a place of healing, a lot of untruthful statements were made about me. Many were attacks against my character and the call on my life. This made starting a ministry very difficult, but in order to have a healing ministry, a foundation of change must happen. It had to start with me. In recognizing this, I needed to learn about my enemy, find it's root and pull it out from the very ground it was planted in. No longer will I allow this root-rot to grow in my heart.

After identifying and naming the cause, I had to release it. These steps were difficult because it meant facing my fears. Looking deep within myself, I started to name each person who caused me pain. Even if it was a minor offense, I still named them. After calling out the name of the individuals, I asked the Lord to forgive their actions and to not hold them accountable for what they done. I then stated to the Lord that I released every one of them and I forgave them. While forgiving the people of their actions, I petitioned the Lord to forgive me of mine as well and to create within me a clean heart and renewed right spirit (Psalms 51:10).

Overcoming The Spirit of Fear

I desire to help others come to a place of forgiveness so they will not experience the consequences of this spiritual arthritis. In the process of my healing, I came to understand it was not people I was fighting, but a spirit operating through people.

For we wrestle not against flesh and blood, but against principalities, against powers, against the rulers of the darkness of this world, against spiritual wickedness in high places. Ephesians 6:12 KJV

The spirit of fear is one of the funguses used by the enemy to uproot God's children out of their rightful secured position in Him. Out of this spirit is birth division, identity theft, disobedience, distrust, jealously and spiritual murder.

The spirit of division is a lie set up by Satan to keep the many ministries from uniting together as one body.

Now I beseech you, brethren, by the name of our Lord Jesus Christ, that ye all speak the same thing, and that there be no divisions among you; but that ye be perfectly joined together in the same mind and in the same judgment. I Corinthians 1:10 KJV

There is great fear among the children of God to not support any ministry that may be outside of the religious culture they are familiar with. This creates a superficial power which controls and monopolizes the minds of the people. This power comes in the form of pride and haughtiness. We separate ourselves because we believe our religion is the only truth.

Satan strategically devised this plan to manipulate and bring a spiritual wedge of distrust between the people of the congregations and the para-church ministries, thus creating a Christian Civil War putting brother against brother, sister against sister, church against church and congregation against congregation. However, we are to be joining forces to fight against the darkness of Satan instead of dividing resources or spiritual revelations to fight one another.

Soon after division and pride follows jealousy. We become envious of one another if one Christian group, church or person succeeds in something we desire to do but for various reasons wouldn't or couldn't do. For example, let's say a very small church starts out with nine members and within a year it grows to be over a two thousand members. Within five years it grows to over six thousand members. What would you think? Would you speak curses over the congregation by saying it's a cult? Would you speak negatively about the pastor when you have never been in the church? Would you begin to question if the uncompromised Word of God was preached in the facility? These are some of the very things I hear when one group is prosperous and another is wanting.

For jealousy is the rage of a man: therefore he will not spare in the day of vengeance (Proverbs 6:34 KJV).

Out of this very rage comes the harsh and criticizing words which once spoken can not be retracted. This produces *Spiritual Murder*. A small part of our belief and trust we may have had in our brothers and sisters dies. This becomes the seed which creates the roots of discord, opposition, war of words and disdain.

They have sharpened their tongues like a serpent; adders' poison is under their lips. Selah (Psalms 140:3 KJV).

Their throat is like an open place of death; with their tongues they have said what is not true: the poison of snakes is under their lips (Romans 3:13 BET).

We purpose in our heart to not validate the authenticity of the power of God in our sisters and brothers of Christ. This then fabricates a mindset of disobedience to the Word of God which has already declared for us to come together speaking and having the same mind with no division among us.

If then there is any comfort in Christ, any help given by love, any uniting of hearts in the Spirit, any loving mercies and pity, make my joy complete by being of the same mind, having the same love, being in harmony and of one mind. Doing nothing through envy or through pride, but with low thoughts of self. Let everyone take others to be better than himself. Not looking everyone to his private good, but keeping in mind the things of others. Let this mind be in you, which was in Christ Jesus...Do all things without protests and arguments, so that you may be holy and gentle, children of God without sin in a twisted and foolish generation, among whom you are seen as lights in the world, offering the word of life (Philippians 2:1-11 & 14-16 BET).

The spirit of fear continues to spread its seeds by breeding *Spiritual Identity Theft*. On one hand we know what the Bible says, but on the other we hear what the world says. We become perplexed about our decisions and how others view us. Distrust, caution, anxiousness and a guarded view determine the way we accept others. Now we no longer know who we are and crave the love and approval of man instead of the justification and establishment of God.

Moreover whom He did predestinate, them He also called: and whom

He called, them He also justified: and whom He justified, them He also glorified (Romans 8:30 KJV).

We do not have to be governed by the spirit of fear. We can live in a state of deliverance, which supercedes all that we know and can imagine. In this place there is peace, joy, wholeness and restoration. We first must forgive and set free the people who may of knowingly or unknowingly hurt us. This in return gives us the gift of freedom, freedom to love, to hope and to give out of our substance.

For ye have not received the spirit of bondage again to fear; but ye have received the spirit of adoption, whereby we cry, Abba, Father (Romans 8:15 KJV)

Spiritual Chemical Warfare

For by thy words thou shalt be justified, and by thy words thou shalt be condemned (Matthew 12:37 KJV).

Satan is the accuser of the brethren. It is not my job to bring judgment, but it is my job to bring revelation and light. If I were to hold these accusations and the pain it caused, I would die spiritually by the chemical warfare of thoughts and words. What do I mean by this? *Spiritual chemical warfare* is the activation of negative thoughts and words which have been sent towards an individual. What we don't realize is we have the power whether we are saved or not, to send thoughts and words into the atmosphere, thereby activating them to carry out the seed that we are planting.

Like *chemical warfare in the natural*, these thoughts are eventually groomed into words which are not seen, but created to cause great destruction. They are carried on the wind to look for its target and pierce the mind of an individual. The wind could be as simple as another person repeating what has been said. In some cases the wind could be what is being said to a group of people who repeat the words to another group of people. This multiplies and unifies the seed so it grows stronger and has the power to destroy.

If a man never makes a slip in his talk, then he is a complete man and able to keep all his body in control. Now if we put bits of iron into horses' mouths so that they may be guided by us, we have complete control of their bodies. And again ships, though they are so great and are moved by violent winds, are turned by a very small guiding-blade, at the impulse of the man who is using it. Even so the tongue is a small part of the body, but it takes credit for great things. How much wood may be lighted by a very little fire! And the tongue is a fire. It is the power of evil placed in our bodies, making all the body unclean, putting the wheel of life on fire, and getting its fire from hell. For every sort of beast and bird and every living thing on earth and in the sea has been controlled by man and is under his authority, but the tongue may not be controlled by man. It is an unresting evil. It is full of the poison of death. With it we give praise to our Lord and Father; and with it we put a curse on men who are made in God's image. Out of the same mouth comes blessing and cursing. My brothers, it is not right for these things to be so...But if you have bitter envy in your heart and the desire to get the better of others, have no pride in this, talking falsely against what is true (James 3:2-14 BET).

When chemical warfare is used they don't send just one container of the chemicals, they send several to make sure the job is done. It is the same with words. The people sending them cannot just make one statement. They usually make several, thereby increasing its potential of accuracy. It then lays embryonic, growing and taking root into the heart of the person to whom it was sent. Once it has taken root it spreads to every part of the individual's mind and body. The person doesn't know what is wrong until they see the individual who has sent the word. There is something about the seed of negative and harming words, that when it reverences its creator, it's activated.

For when they speak great swelling words of vanity, they allure through the lusts of the flesh, through much wantonness. Those that were clean escaped from them who live in error. Saying that they will be free, while they themselves are the servants of destruction, because whatever gets the better of a man makes a servant of him (2 Peter 2:18-19 BET).

Everything in creation has a master. God of course is the

Master of the Universe, but there is a reason He says there will be no other gods before me (*Exodus 20:3*). Masters are any person, place or thing, which has rule over any person, place or thing. For example, food can be a master when it is the only thing you think about. It causes you to obey its lure to eat. Sickness can be a master if you indulge in the victim mentality of being sick. You empower it to rule over you because you raise it up in your mind as the core part of your psyche. Therefore words are obedient to its creator.

This brings me to another point. We give words power when we allow them to rule over us. Most servants' goal is to eventually be the master. Once the words have been obedient, they become the controlling master of its target. Thereby, being in the forefront of your mind all day and night long. They consume your very intellect and rise up in your spirit to have dominion over your entire life. In so doing they make you the servant to the words and the creator of the words.

Seeing is a gateway often used by the enemy to deceive and to wreak disorder in the spirit. Now the substance of the word comes to surface, butchering the very outlook of the person and taking a stronghold in the person's life. Unforgiveness develops, hatred, mistrust, envy, dislike and corruption, all come towards the portico of the individual's consciousness. A place at the table of your life has been set for the enemy. Satan can come in and manipulate and administrate confusion without any resistance from the person who has received this silent killer. It is medically documented that this soundless assassin is the root for most illnesses, such as heart disease, arthritis, headaches, chronic fatigue and chronic pain among others.

Death and life are in the power of the tongue and they that love it shall eat the fruit thereof (Proverbs 18:21).

Whoso keepeth his mouth and his tongue keepeth his soul from troubles (Proverbs 21:3).

The only antibiotic is the Word of God. This is the shield that renews and protects the mind and the heart. Thoughts, words and viewpoints cannot break through the seal of the Holy Ghost when you read the Word on a daily and continuous basis.

Wherefore take unto you the whole armor of God that ye may be able to withstand in the evil day, and having done all, to stand. Stand therefore, having your loins girt about with truth, and having on the breastplate of righteousness, and your feet shod with the preparation of the gospel of peace. Above all, taking the shield of faith, wherewith ye shall be able to quench all the fiery darts of the wicked. And take the helmet of salvation, and the sword of the Spirit, which is the Word of God. Praying always with all prayer and supplication in the Spirit, and watching thereunto with all perseverance and supplication for all saints...(Ephesians 6:13-17)

The test of forgiveness doesn't just happen overnight, but is a continuous level of privilege. It is an advantage as well as benefit to forgive. It is also a process. The Bible says: *But we all, with unveiled face giving back as in a glass the glory of the Lord, are changed into the same image from glory to glory, even as from the Lord who is the Spirit (2 Corinthians 3:18 BET).*

This scripture is a prime example of progression. We are changed into His image from glory to glory. The test of character begins with the answer of forgiveness.

The Ultimate Challenge

Before I go any further, let me break down the difference between quizzes, tests and exams. I believe as we progress from glory to glory the tests progress from quizzes to exams.

Quizzes are those nuisances that pop up to see if you really got what you just heard from your pastor or teacher. A teacher can be anything from an experience with an individual to an actual mentor and or the Holy Spirit.

An example of a quiz is you just heard a word about forgiveness from your church. You finally think you have it locked down in your spirit. Suddenly, an old acquaintance whom you haven't seen in twenty years shows up at the grocery store and is now standing right behind you. You begin to remember all the lies this individual has spread about you and now you are faced with a decision. Do you speak or do you ignore them? Thus the quiz. The very word you just received within the last few moments of your life gets quizzed immediately. This decision will actually take you to the next level of discipline if you answer correctly.

An example of a test is you have now gone through a season where nothing but prosperity has come your way. Prophecy and confirmation seems to be an everyday occurrence. You're built up in your spirit. Your strong and wise, because good has been what you have seen all this time. Suddenly without warning, stuff starts happening at your job. You can't seem to do anything right. To top it off, you go home and the family seems to be in disarray. You become alarmed and start to back track and repeat your steps to see if you are in the will of God or if you have grieved the Holy Spirit. You begin to search the Word for answers. You call out on Jesus for understanding and He is silent. Thus the test. Do you complain, get angry, feel betrayed or do you remember the prophecies which have been coming consistently and hold on tight to the Word you received? This decision will be the deciding course of action for the next few time spans of your life. If you choose your emotions over the Word of God, you will take the same test over and over and over again until you get it right. However, if you stand on the Word of God, you will have peace that passes all understanding and you can't help but give Him praise in the midst of the test. (Philippians 4:7)

Now exams are different. I believe exams combine all the tests and quizzes you have gone through for the ultimate challenge of reaching the next dimension in God. Exams last longer than test. This is the time of the fire. This is what the Bible calls a trial. It really is the time where Satan asks to place you on trial. This is the ultimate challenge. To be squeezed and crushed so you can come out like fine wine. Exams test your spirit, your character, your knowledge, your flesh, your will and your faith.

It is in this period of stillness where you determine if you will go on towards the prize of Jesus or remain dormant in your current state of revelation. It's a time of seeking, searching and understanding. Like school, exams can be very complicated when you are not properly prepared or very simple when the principles of what you have learned are applied.

My exam began in 2002. I was diagnosed with *fibromyalgia*. This disease crippled my body in ways, which are unexplainable. In my body every muscle ached. Fibromyalgia has many elements. Heartburn, unbearable headaches, dizziness, not being able to judge distance, coldness to the bones, uncontrollable bed wetting, stiffness in the joints, unstable equilibrium, chest pains and tightness among other things are triggered and carried out when the illness is fully activated. Anything can activate the illness from a slight change in weather to a small bump against a table. When the doctor diagnosed me with this disease, I wanted to cry. I waited until I reached my van and just let it all out. I asked God why. "Why Lord would You allow me to come through hell to go through this?" It didn't stop there, within two months after being diagnosed with fibromyalgia, I was diagnosed with lumbar disc disease, rheumatoid arthritis, calcium on my brain, irritable bowl syndrome, periodontal disease, cysts on my ovaries and on my liver, all at once. These were the many facets of fibromyalgia.

When the members of the clergy heard about the illness I was diagnosed with, some said to me "You must have sinned. Illness only comes from sinning." The best statement said by a minister was "Your faith is extremely weak, there must be something wrong with your faith. Surely, God would deliver you if you had enough faith."

My spirit and soul became vexed. There was no peace in my spirit. I became concerned about the medical bills that were piling up. I had to see my doctor three times a week. I was on twenty-six different medications and receiving trigger point injections in my neck which totaled twenty-five a month. Because of the medications I was on, my weight went from 145 pounds to 162 pounds. I no longer felt attractive. I was at my weakest state physically and mentally. Finally, I called out like an infant. I didn't have the words to approach God's throne. All I could do was cry. Scriptures began to flood my spirit. The cries got louder but were transformed into scriptures.

No weapon formed against me shall prosper Isaiah 54:17.

Surely, goodness and mercy shall follow me all the days of my life and I will dwell in the house of the Lord forever Psalms 23:6.

From the end of the earth will I cry unto Thee, when my heart is overwhelmed, lead me to the rock that is higher than I Psalms 61:2.

I will praise the name of God with a song, and will magnify Him with thanksgiving Psalms 69:30.

But he was wounded for our transgressions, He was bruised for our iniquities, the chastisement of our peace was upon Him and with His stripes we are healed Isaiah 53:5.

These scriptures came out of my spirit and joy replaced the grief I was carrying. Now the pain became my strength. It was my testimony. When I ministered, I would share with people the miracle of being able to sing in the midst of the pain and the miracle of being able to praise God in the midst of being crippled. I made up in my heart I will praise God in the situation as well as out of the situation.

This went on from 2002 -2003. In 2003 at the *Ladies Night Out Conference*, God told me to take all of my pill bottles with me. I was to speak on *A Kept Woman*. After I was finished with the message, the Holy Spirit directed me to pour all of my medicine bottles on the floor and step on them. As I did, the Holy Spirit began to prophecy to me and I said out loud to the congregation, nothing will have the authority to overcome or deceive me again. You see, in the beginning, the serpent approached Eve to talk and deceive her. In the natural when a serpent is ready to strike, it raises its head from the ground to

A Kept Woman

get a better aim at its victim. God spoke to Eve and made a covenant with her stating her seed would have the victory.

And the Lord God said to the snake, Because you have done this you are cursed more than all cattle and every beast of the field; **you will go flat on the earth, and dust will be your food all the days of your life:** *And there will be* **war between you and the woman** *and between your seed and her seed: by Him (Christ) will your head be crushed and by you his foot will be wounded. (Genesis 3: 14 BET)*

This covenant allowed me to claim my victory. The serpent, which represents any deceptive, manipulating spirit or circumstance, will not have rule over me. God cursed the serpent to the ground thereby guaranteeing my victory. After my proclamation of stepping on the medicine, I never took another pill. Now, because I did this does not mean you should do the same. The Holy Spirit guided me on what to do. I believe there are doctors who are ordained by God to carry out His work in medicine. If you feel as if your spirit is unctioning you to do this, please judge the spirit by the Spirit. Satan can easily come as light. Do not be deceived.

After stopping the medication, I went back to my doctor. Miracle after miracle happened. The cysts which were on my liver and ovaries were gone. The doctors were bewildered and continued to take tests to try and prove their other tests were correct. When examined again for lumbar disc disease, the doctor found new cartilage in my vertebra and could not detect any rheumatoid arthritis. They said that I had a back of a twelve year old. This was a miracle. Cartilage cannot grow back. The periodontal disease that was sending poison to my heart was no more. The periodontal dentist could not believe that the bone in my teeth grew back. My gum lines were perfect and regained their muscle strength. The fibromyalgia still flares up, but not the way it used to. God has given me the strength to do whatever He desires for me to do. I don't allow this illness to control my functioning capacity or me but I control it. I am at a place of rest.

Please understand this does not mean I accept the illness. I claim everything the Word of God says is mine. Anything that is against what the Word says, I do not accept. I am completely healed and it is only a matter of time before it is manifested. Meanwhile, I am at peace with His decisions governing me. Let me go on to say God is not about magic. This was not magic that healed my body of all these ailments, but the complete trust in the Word of God. Though it concerned me when I was diagnosed, peace dwelled in my mind and my spirit because I already had Jesus living on the inside of me. I was not lacking in His grace or His love and I was found by the court of the High King to be innocent of the charges Satan accused me of.

This was a place of ultimate trust. Just as my own children would ask of me knowing without any doubt I will provide for their every need, this same level of trust is what I had to have in order to believe God.

Faith comes by hearing, and hearing by the Word of God *(Romans 10:17)*. I'm not talking about hope, for hope is wishing it might happen, but faith. A faith so intense and so at peace, that just a glimpse of it moves all mountains and gives you dominion over all principalities. This type of faith is obtained by fasting and praying.

And He saith unto them, because of your little faith: for verily I say unto you, If ye have faith as a grain of mustard seed, ye shall say unto this mountain, remove hence to yonder place; and it shall remove; and nothing shall be impossible unto you. But this kind goeth not out save by prayer and fasting (Matthew 17:20-21).

By fasting and praying you build a relationship with your Father. You spend time submitting and breaking spiritual bread with your Daddy. The more you want to please Him, the more He is pleased.

The Bible clearly states that faith without works is dead.

What doth it profit, my brethren, if a man say he hath faith, but have not works? Can that faith save him? If a brother or sister be naked and in lack of daily food, and one of you say unto them, Go in peace, be ye warmed and filled; and yet ye give them not the things needful to the body; what doth it profit? Even so faith, if it has not works, is dead in itself (James 2:14-17).

My works were fasting, praying and believing. These actions triggered a reaction of building and maintaining closeness with my Father.

Building anything takes a foundation of some form of strong substance. To build a solid relationship with God, I had to start with the first brick of faith. I had to have faith to believe that He is. Upon this brick was the ability to stack other bricks that had the ingredients of faith. This stacking of peace, hope, endurance and longsuffering moved me to new levels of trust.

Now faith is the substance of things hoped for, the evidence of things not seen (Hebrew 11:1).

I didn't walk around looking or acting defeated, nor was I speaking in a language of defeat just because I was being attacked. Yes, the punches were hard. They were hard on my body and on my mind. But my spirit is more than a conqueror. I didn't live through my past to get to this exam and fail. If anything, now I have a *her-story*, which provided proof that my Father will meet my needs. If He could answer me when I did not know Him, how much more will He answer now that I am intimate with Him? This was not the time to give up, but the correct moment to activate my faith, stand on the firm foundation of His Word and believe the impossible to be possible.

I have learned during this exam, in all things to give Him thanks. The Bible says, *Let everything that has breath, praise ye the Lord (Psalms 150:6).* As long as there is breath in my body, I will praise the Lord. Even when I can't speak I will praise the Lord with my obedience to His will in my life.

Intimate Worship

Overcoming these illnesses taught me compassion. They also taught me to never take life or people for granted. It became easier to see people in their moments of need and help them.

During the time span of these illnesses, God strategically placed me to work at a dialysis clinic. Here I was in pain, yet, I had to be a counselor to some of my colleagues and patients. The lesson to learn was to keep on serving in the midst of your trial. There is always someone who is carrying a bigger load than you. I faced death and heartache as an everyday occurence at this facility. It allowed me put everything into perspective.

In learning a lot about healing, I have found there are many different levels of healing. Sometimes as Christians, we desire to see the flesh healed. We stop short of desiring and acknowledging the soul being healed.

One example of this is a patient I had at the dialysis clinic. She had diabetes and was dying. Her fingers, what was left of them, were black and rotting off her hand. She had only one leg, which was decaying from gangrene. She was not very clean and looked horrible. Because of the pain she was suffering, she was on several medications. These medications kept her asleep. When she would come to dialysis, the nurse would have to lift her up to place in the chair. After dialysis, they would shake her to get her awake. I watched this happen for a couple of months. I would weigh her in and then push her over to her seat. One day as I was weighing her the Holy Spirit said "Take your hands and wipe them through her hair and kiss her forehead." I replied, "What? This woman is filthy". However, I did what the Spirit said. Once I touched her hair, my repulsion subsided and my heart was filled with love for her. I bent down and kissed her forehead and whispered, "In Jesus Name, give her peace." She was still asleep when I pushed her wheelchair out to the foyer. Tears were in my eyes as I watched her. I didn't understand at the time what God was doing, but I do know He changed my heart in order to bless her.

She returned on Wednesday a different woman. She had on lipstick and nice clothes and was fully awake. I was shocked by the transformation. "Wow, Lord" I said, "You are healing her." Everyone in the place could not believe this was the same woman. I stayed quiet about what happened since it was not about me. When I went to push her out to the foyer she said to me "Lynnette, was it you who kissed me Monday?" I looked at her and said, "No, it was Jesus". She smiled at me and said, "I thank Him". This was the last time I saw her alive. I received word she died while she was sleeping. I ran to the back kitchen because I didn't understand. I was devastated by the news. "Lord" I cried, "Why did you have me touch her and then not heal her?" The Lord responded as quickly as I asked. "Lynnette, I did heal her. I gave her what she requested. I gave her peace."

Healing is not always the way I think or man thinks it should be. This moment in my life led me to write a song on her behalf and escorted me to the next part of ministry in my life.

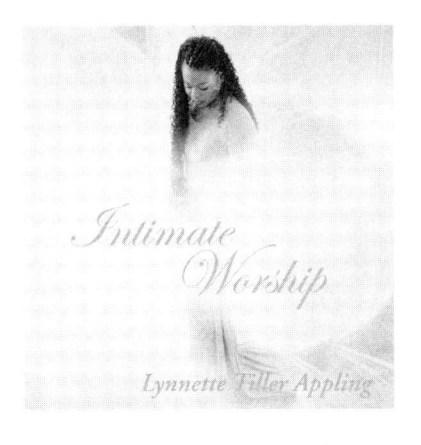

This particular song, which became my anthem and many other women's song of praise, is entitled *Beyond the Veil*.

So many days, my soul is tired
My tears are hard to hide
This broken heart of mine,
In it no love can hide.
How do I say help me?
How can I survive this pain?
There's no one who truly knows me,
Please tell me my name.
My body aches everyday.
I search for kindness in someone's face.

> *I hear whispers behind my back,*
> *Testing me, trying me, saying it's faith that I lack.*
> *How do I tell you of my loneliness?*
> *I'm broken in spirit and I need time to heal.*
> *I need to fall at God's feet*
> *And go beyond the veil*
> *Where my healing can begin*
> *I need to know where I end and He begins.*
> *If I just press my way through and go*
> *Beyond the veil*
> *I need to go where the healing balm is.*
> *A special place where I can find my strength within*
> *In His arms, I know I can hide, fly high on His wings.*
> *In His presence, it's in His presence where I must abide.*
> *At His throne, I will find peace, hope and love,*
> *Beyond the veil.*

These collections of songs became my second CD entitled *Intimate Worship*. There is one song that has become one of my favorites to sing when I think the quizzes, test and exams are just a little hard and that song is *Father*.

> *Father, as I life my voice and call out on Your name*
> *It's Your face I seek and grace that has not changed*
> *I need to hide in You.*
> *Hear me as I pray to find out Your will*
> *Crucify my flesh and teach me how to kneel*
> *Forgive my selfish zeal*
> *I don't want to be about me*
> *I just want to know Your heart*
> *Allow me to sit at Your feet and know the love of Your arms*
> *And know the love Your arms.*
> *Father let me be the vessel that You can use*
> *Search my heart and see if it is true*
> *I surrender my life to You*
> *I don't want it to be about me*
> *I just want to know Your heart*
> *Allow me to wipe my tears at Your feet*

And know the love of Your arms,
And know the love of Your arms.

I craved Him. I yearned for His mindset. There was so much I didn't understand and I didn't have to. Sometimes in this life, it's nice to just be. Be still in Him. Be what you are created to be. I worshipped His awesomeness and His simplicity of being God. I was secure in knowing He is the Almighty. God is immeasurable and incalculable. No matter what else I may go through during these times of testing, quizzes or exams, He is the great and merciful I AM. Because Christ is my source, resource and place of rest, I am learning like Paul to be content in all things and for His grace is sufficient.

And he said to me, My grace is enough for you, for My power is made complete in what is feeble. Most gladly, then, will I take pride in my feeble body, so that the power of Christ may be on me. So I take pleasure in being feeble, in unkind words, in needs, in cruel attacks, in troubles, on account of Christ: for when I am feeble, then am I strong (2 Corinthians 12:9-10 BET).

Not that I speak in respect of want: for I have learned, in whatsoever state I am, therewith to be content. I know both how to be abased, and I know how to abound: everywhere and in all things I am instructed both to be full and to be hungry, both to abound and to suffer need. I can do all things through Christ, which strengthened me (Philippians 4:11-13).

Lynnette Tiller Appling

A Kept Woman

Epoch 3

Lynnette Tiller Appling

Understanding With Wisdom

My mouth shall speak of wisdom; and the meditation of my heart shall be of understanding.
Psalms 49:3

The fear of the Lord is the beginning of wisdom and the knowledge of the Holy is understanding.
Proverbs 9:10

A wise man will hear, and will increase learning; and a man of understanding shall attain unto wise counsels.
Proverbs 1:5

Wisdom is the principal thing; therefore get wisdom: and with all thy getting get understanding.
Proverbs 4:7

Lynnette Tiller Appling

Discerning His Heart

My mouth shall speak of wisdom; and the meditation of my heart shall be of understanding (Psalms 49:3).

I was driving down Dressler Road in a hurry to get to work when I looked around and saw the state of the area. The clouds were gray and hanging very low. The birds were not flying, and sprinkles of rain drizzled on the passing cars and houses. As I slowed down, I felt a form of heaviness. I pulled the van over and asked the Lord what it was. All of a sudden, I remembered this was the first anniversary of 9/11. As I remembered the unforgettable day, the heaviness became more prevalent. I actually could hear crying in the air. I closed my eyes and put my arms around myself as I began to rock back and forth.

The nation was mourning. I could hear the weeping. I opened my eyes and cried out to the Lord and said, "What can I do for you father?" He replied, "Remind them that I love them." The weeping and wailing became louder. I almost could not bear the sound. I heard children crying for their parents, wives morning their husbands and families praying for peace. God allowed me to hear what He hears. I opened my mouth and screamed as loud as I could, because my heart was breaking from the load of their pain, and cried "I will do whatever You ask of me Father to help Your people." The sounds stopped, but my heart could feel the emptiness in the land. My breathing was rapid. My heart was pounding. I looked to see if anyone saw me. I turned the key to the ignition slowly giving me time to catch my breath, started up the van and went to work.

This event made me keenly aware of my surroundings. No longer do I just rush to my destination, but I seek out His heart and asked Him daily what I can do for Him.

Time with Him is not to be taken for granted or used half heartily. It must be cherished and used wisely. It is such a precious gift. Once it has passed it does not come again. You cannot make it up or gain it back.

The person who said time is on your side did not understand what time it was. You must always consider the cost of anything before you try it, however, utilize every second and make every minute count by giving God glory in your life. This includes learning to have a day of rest. This is worship to Him to be able to be obedient and rest. Become skilled at enjoying and recognizing true life, not by the world's standards, but by God's ordinance. Make up in your mind and heart that your time will be used doing the will of the Lord. In doing so, you will understand His heart.

Little Twiggy

Many people ask me questions on how to deal with different situations. Some of the phone calls I receive are handled with the same revelation called *Little Twiggys*.

Little Twiggys are issues blown up to be crosses, when in reality they are two twigs put together, tied in the middle and made to look like a cross. There are several different types of twigs we combine together and then struggle to make them into something of worth. We fail to comprehend twigs are fallen, broken pieces of a tree. Without a source of life or grounded roots, they will die. Some twigs are already dead, yet we endeavor to keep them alive.

We can't nail anything on the twigs, nevertheless, we pray to it, bow to it and think it is actually going to get God's attention. Some of us wear them around our necks so others can see them and have great reverence for our suffering. Instead of taking our twigs to the cross, we create our own crosses with the twigs. These twigs have no power. There is no bloodstain running down them to cover our sins. Still, somehow we believe these twigs are heavy enough to get some consideration and place us in right standing with God. These twigs are trivial and make us self-righteous.

We all have little twiggys in our life, frivolous hang-ups we carry with us all the time. For example, some of us are apprehensive because someone has on red nail polish. For some unknown and unfounded reason, nail color offends you. Because of this you condemn everyone who wears it to burn in hell. Or better yet, if the hem of someone's skirt is shorter than one inch above the ankle, a woman is a harlot and after all the married men in the church. Another example is, if a speaker has on a gorgeous robe, some say *it's too much because you can't concentrate on what she is saying because of the outfit. Surely, the speaker should consider this so she can be accepted and listened to. Besides, it's not about her. She will do well to remember this.* Funny how female speakers talk about other females' clothing, but I never hear this statement said about men.

You gather your little twiggys together and take them to the throne room to offer your sacrifice. You asked the Lord to accept the offering you are bringing to Him, not realizing your twiggys don't have enough friction to even make a fire. Even if they did manage to hold a fire, the fire will only last for a few seconds. They turn into splinters at the very look from God because they can't hold ground.

My suggestion to this problem is to gather all your twigs together, build a bonfire, and burn them. It's time out for us condemning one another because of our own hang-ups and unbiblical beliefs. If God told you not to wear red nail polish, then don't do it, but don't judge the other person because they are wearing it. If you wear your skirts to the floor, don't say someone is not holy because they have on a skirt to the middle of their kneecap. If someone has on a sharp robe or clothing, don't make it her problem because of a jealous, unrepentant heart. When you walk in a spirit of spitefulness, you are not be able to receive the Word God has for you.

There comes a time when you should not sweat the small things. It is the small things that destroy the vine (Solomon 2:15). I am not saying to overlook sin, but when it is not sin, don't become wayward in your behavior or in the way you view things. Remember, everything is not what it seems and perception can be deceiving. Red fingernail polish is not going to send anyone to hell, skirts will not create a place in hell, and sharp robes do not kindle the fire in hell. Allow God to judge and discipline His children.

Seasonal Acquaintances and Lifetime Friends

This lesson was one I had to learn with my friends. If I was to be a friend to them and them to me, I had to accept them where they were and encourage them to strive higher and vise versa. I couldn't condemn them for not having some of the revelations God had given me. It didn't make me greater than them because I knew and they didn't. It actually made me a servant. Because of the revelation God entrusted me with, I had to get it to the people. If they are not ready for meat, how could I serve it? It had to be broken down into sizes they could digest. This process is servanthood. Serving keeps me humble and reminds me to burn my twigs daily.

I started to have wisdom in proper treatment of God's children. They were never to feel inferior to anyone, most of all God's people. It is only by grace we are saved. I have no special connection others can't have. Everyone has the same way of passage to His throne. It is the process of implementation, obedience and how you apply the principles of His Word that teaches us how to get there. This is what makes some of us quicker learners than others.

This progression also separates us from people who are seasonal in our lives. I have had many acquaintances, but only a few lifetime friends. These friends are partners with me throughout every moment in my life. It deeply hurt me to see the seasonal acquaintances come and go at first. But as I grew in wisdom of progression, I understood the development of the seasons. Each term was a specific time in my life to be expanded upon. I knew iron sharpens iron *(Proverbs 27:1)* and perfect love casts out all fear *(I John 4:18)*. Knowing this helped me to overcome my inhibitions of moving on.

With deep love, I cherish my lifetime friends. They are the type of people you can speak to once a year and it's like you never missed a beat. One special friend has been in my life since I was thirteen years old. *Renee' Meeks* became a God-sent friend when I was twenty. She came into my life without me asking for her. She was there during my first marriage and she watched me struggle with the death of my son. Renee' is a witness to the pain and disruption which was in my life. She held my hand when I learned how to drive at the age of twenty-three. She took care of my daughter Shaila when my first husband dropped her off and left her for over a week in her care.

Renee' was there during my many abusive relationships, through the tears, the anger, the misconceptions. Not one time did she judge me or condemn me for not knowing who I was. Instead, we had coffee or tea and talked about the goodness of the Lord.

When she went through almost the same scenario a few years later, it was my turn to be there for her. Not judging, not condemning, but understanding. She lives in Columbus, Ohio and when the Lord tells her to call, she does and visa versa. We see each other maybe once or, if we are really blessed, twice a year.

Now Renee' is in my life during the blessings and the celebration of who God created me to be. She was there in the past and now she shares my future, praying and holding my hand through thick and thin. I truly love this woman of God, a warrior and a God-sent friend.

It is very rare to have friends like this who truly accept you as you are. Most people immediately try to change you and turn you into their likeness. I too have tried to do this very same thing. It really is a wonderful journey to the road of truth when you have lifetime God-sent friends in your life. They don't distract you, or try to be you, but they enhance who you are and grow as you do.

Seasonal acquaintances depend on what season you are in. When it's harvest time you will always have someone saying they are close to you and they have your back. But when winter comes the phone barely rings and people keep their distance. Get popular in the summer and they all come out to play. During the springtime of your life they watch to see if you are going to have seed to plant before they decide to be your friend. They come and go as the wind. Nevertheless, their time has some purpose of growth for you.

I have had people who have stayed close to me in order to mimic the same knowledge I have gained to further themselves. There are friends I have experienced who desired more from me than what I could give. There have been many people in my life I have been a friend to and they have been an acquaintance to me. These people used me as a resource to get their needs met. For this reason, I have learned to let these contacts be a point of wisdom by gaining knowledge of their devices and guarding my heart.

Wisdom dictates and mandates that you know yourself and the people who are on the boat with you. In the same sense, you must also be aware of where your boat is docked. Being knowledgeable about your environment and each gateway is crucial to your spiritual walk.

The Last Mile

Near the end of 2003, the Lord brought me to the very place in which this story began... me being fatherless.

I was asleep on Friday, October 17, when the phone rang around 2:30 in the morning. For the last five years I wondered when the phone rang if the person on the other end was going to tell me my father had passed away. The sound of the ring became muffled. It rang like this so many times before with the voice on the other end telling me my father was in the hospital fighting for his life. I'd pack up my family to rush to be by his side. In spite of that I knew he would survive. But this ring was different. I got up from the bed, picked up the phone and said "Hello." "Mrs. Appling", the voice said discouraged, "Your father was rushed to Grant Hospital. He is on life support. We had to revive him." I waited and hesitated to respond. "Thank you for calling, I will come down in the morning." I hung up the phone and went back to bed. There was a peace which surpassed even my understanding.

I awakened around 7:00 a.m., prepared the children and began to meditate on the Lord. Unexpectedly, my heart flooded with emotions. I grabbed my chest and fell to my knees by my bed. Without me wanting to, I knew I would be the one everyone leaned on.

As I began to cry, the voice of the Lord said to me "Lynnette I have already taken him. You must prepare to speak at his funeral." For the first time in my life I said to the Lord "No, not me. I can't bury him and speak. Find someone else, allow me to just be the daughter." As I was saying this to Him, Jeffery came into the room and said "God has said that you are to speak at your father's funeral. You must prepare." My heart sank at the mere thought of my father being gone.

We arrived in Columbus at Grant Hospital around 11:00 a.m. on October 18, 2003. My sister Mary was already there. We were the only ones. I looked at her and asked how father was doing. She responded, "He looks tired." I walked into my father's room. He opened his eyes and mouthed the words "I love you." I took a cold wet towel and wiped his forehead. As I was rubbing his head, I sang to him any melody that would come to my heart. Everyone thought he was getting better. However, I knew he was already gone and what we were experiencing was just a shell of what God had already said was done.

My father was tired and worn out. His body was crippled and twisted up so much he looked like a pretzel. I could tell he had enough of life. He'd been fighting this illness since he was thirty-one years old. I remember the first time we saw the illness manifested. My sister and I were staying at his house for the weekend. I was around eleven years old, my sister was about seven and my little brother was just a baby. Daddy came to the top of the stairs to speak to me. He tumbled down the steps like a bouncing ball. I was so frightened for him. He was shaking uncontrollably. As the illness progressed, holding a cup of coffee was a chore for him. He became frustrated and angry over his illness because now he was dependent on someone else. His anger made him abusive to his current wife. I understood him. I too was angry he got sick. I felt as though it robbed me of any time we could have shared. At that age of course I thought if he would of just stayed with me none of this would of happened. It was during this time of searching and complete dependency that my father sought out God. He became an ordained minister and from what I was told, he could really preach.

As I watched my father fight for his breaths, I realized everything I used to feel was gone. I wasn't empty or ashamed to be his daughter anymore. There was no stigma in loving him, nor did I need to hide my deep love for him. It's a funny thing about death, people become free to love again because there's nothing to lose and everything to gain.

I had come full circle standing beside his hospital bed, wiping his brow and kissing his chapped lips. I was back in love with my father. The very road that took us on separate journeys, led us both to each other. Now near the end of his road, I would be there to walk the last mile with him.

I called the family to let them know he only had a couple of days to a week to live. They came to the hospital and really believed he was going to rise up and walk. My grandmother could not release him to go. I didn't want to fight with her, since I understood the love a mother has for her son. So I stayed silent and allowed her to keep her hope.

They put my father in hospice care for his last remaining days on earth. No one wanted to make decisions about his care. My family thought they were killing my father. I stepped up to the plate. I had a little medical knowledge, and I had dealt with death in ways no one in the room had experienced. Making every decision for him, I fought for his comfort and was his voice.

My little brother and I stayed with my father the rest of the week. I would get up at 5:00 a.m. and go to the hospital and stay until 1:00 a.m. the next day. My family members came late in the evening. They were still hoping against hope he would be okay. The only thought I had was I would not allow my daddy to die alone.

On that Thursday, my father opened his eyes and looked towards the heavens. A peaceful presence was in the room. He was asking for something, but not from any of us. Whoever he saw, was whom he was talking to. That's when I knew his personal escort was an angel.

A Kept Woman

My father never complained one time near the end of his illness. All he wanted was his Bible and the TV. He loved cartoons. I learned so much from watching him during this time. He was at peace. Each day I sat alone in a chair watching my father slip away. It was symbolic that we were at this point in our relationship. When daddy left the first time I watched and counted the seconds praying against hope he would see the love in my eyes and stay. I knew he would be back and he would have some form of existence in my life. This time I was watching him leave forever and I was okay with it. It did not hurt me anymore. I had no hatred towards him, no ill wishes. All I had was love for him. My deepest desire for my father was for him to be surrounded by love. What's ironic is my love was the very thing he gave up so long ago. Now, I was able to freely give it back to him, unrestrained, uninhibited and pure. This was our time and this was my gift.

On Friday the Lord told me to go back to Canton and return to Columbus on Saturday. I kissed my father one last time and informed the nurses of what I was doing. I called my little brother and told him to get to the hospital to sit with Dad. When I got back home, I was tired. I took Garra to a friend's birthday party and came back home. Exhausted, I laid across my bed to get some rest. My heart began to slow down and my breathing became shallow. This is when I sensed Daddy was leaving this world. Quickly, I jumped up and called the hospital. They informed me that my father's blood pressure was 58 over Doppler. My brother put dad on the phone. "Daddy", I said, "If you want to rest, then go. We will be okay. I love you Daddy." He tried to respond, and I knew what he was trying to say. "I love you too" I said, "Now rest Daddy, rest." I slowly hung up the phone and shut my eyes. There was no need to count anymore, this time he was not coming back.

Saturday October 25, 2003 at 9:00 a.m., my father at age 57, left this world and all his physical pain behind. I planned his funeral and honored my father accordingly and respectfully. For his eulogy I spoke about forgiveness. I didn't speak about my father's great achievements or conquest as everyone thought

I would. Instead, I spoke on letting go of the pain and becoming a family of peace and love.

As they lowered his casket into the ground, I turned around to say goodbye. My eyes did not want to leave the place in which his body was laid to rest. With tears clouding my eyes, I whispered to myself as I took one last look and proudly said, "I am Lynnette Raye Tiller, the daughter and blessed seed of James William Tiller, Sr."

Giving Up The Call

Wisdom is the principal thing; therefore get wisdom: and with all thy getting get understanding. Proverbs 4:7

During the seasons of one's life, one must learn not to regret. You must always learn, but don't regret. For each moment is another building block of your character and your wisdom. During the time spans of my life I did question my purpose. Though you may know what your purpose is, the flesh may sometimes question whether it is real.

I am not writing this book to give you a rosy picture of how everything worked out. The fact is, life is work and living takes work. There is so much to consider, to forgive and to be careful of. There is no way you can keep all of it straight. But getting caught up in the dos and don'ts and only concentrating on these facets are the traps and chains of living by the law and not by grace.

It was just one week after my father's death and I had to prepare myself for ministry once again. I couldn't cancel the concert because it was too late. So I went forward not giving myself time to properly mourn the death of my father.

I pushed myself too hard on top of the death of my father. The pieces of my father's life had fallen and for some reason they fell at my feet. Family members called continuously for counseling and comfort. This was not something I was responsible for, nor could I give the understanding and compassion that under normal circumstances I would have given. The only duty I had was to lead them to the *heart fixer*. The only way I could do this was to tell them to pray for themselves. I left the pieces there.

After the rush of the funeral and the concert, my life became silent. I had to step back and regroup. There were many days I felt out of sorts. I became angry at life. Neither my husband nor my children could fill the void and emptiness I felt. Frustration set in to my soul. I thought this was part of the mourning process for my father, but it was much more. It went deeper. I didn't want to do ministry anymore. This was not like before. Something changed in me. I'd been working in the ministry for a long time. I was a leader of many. Even my family pushed me to the forefront of being a leader. I saw so much, did so much, gave so much and now I was tired. My heart was exhausted from holding people up. I was pouring a significant portion of my spirit out with nothing pouring back in. I became quiet and withdrawn. There was bitterness because no one seemed to care that his or her problems depleted me. I had not been taught yet about being an intercessor. Because of this lack of understanding and wisdom, the people's cares became my property. I gave and gave and gave... and at this point there was nothing more to give. This wasn't depression or self pity, it was a simple case of burn out.

I began to talk to God. I opened up in a way I've never done before. This was not the time for eloquent words or superficial phrases. I needed a touch from Him. I cried from the depths of my soul. Wailing from the tips of my toes to the ends of my hair. Every part of my spirit ached with spiritual pain.

"Lord, I can't do it anymore. I know that You called me. I understand that You love me, but I am so very tired. These people have taken the last drop of water I had. I am dry and broken. Lord if there is any other way You can take away this call, please do."

As soon as I spoke out these words, the Holy Ghost began to comfort me. He explained the call is given without repentance and is irreversible. He guided me to Romans 8:26-30 (BET).

And in the same way the Spirit is a help to our feeble hearts: for we are not able to make prayer to God in the right way; but the Spirit puts our desires into words which are not in our power to say; And He who is the searcher of hearts has knowledge of the mind of the Spirit, because He is making prayers for the saints in agreement with the mind of God. And we are conscious that all things are working together for good to those who have love for God, and have been marked out by His purpose... Moreover whom He did predestinate, them He also called: and whom He called, them He also justified: and whom He justified, them He also glorified. What shall we then say to these things? If God be for us, who can be against us? Who shall lay any thing to the charge of God's elect? It is God that justifies. Who is he that condemns? It is Christ that died, yea rather, that is risen again, who is even at the right hand of God, who also maketh intercession for us. Who shall separate us from the love of Christ? Shall tribulation, or distress, or persecution, or famine, or nakedness, or peril, or sword? As it is written, for Thy sake we are killed all the daylong; we are accounted as sheep for the slaughter

Nay, in all these things we are more than conquerors through Him that loved us. For I am persuaded, that neither death, nor life, nor angels, nor principalities, nor powers, nor things present, nor things to come, Nor height, nor depth, nor any other creature, shall be able to separate us from the love of God, which is in Christ Jesus our Lord.

I repented for my self-absorbed thinking. I kept reading the scripture over and over again until it penetrated my heart and my mind. I started to praise God in tongues until it became worship. The Spirit of God spoke to the Holy Spirit in me and the Holy Spirit gave Him my report.

The Word of God is life. It is living. It breathes into the very spirit of man and speaks to that which is dead to live. By the time the Holy Ghost was through with me, I was refreshed, strong and quickened.

The Power of Spiritual Mothers

A wise man will hear, and will increase learning; and a man of understanding shall attain unto wise counsels (Proverbs 1:5).

It wasn't long after this the Lord sent me someone who would teach and guide me. This wonderful woman has taken the time out of her schedule to be my spiritual mother. I know she has been handpicked by God to do this because when she corrects me, I receive it with humility and understanding and I make the changes.

The glory of God rests on her shoulders and His power is demonstrated through her. She travels the world and has seen many nations change. I sit at her feet, listen to her tapes, read her books, have intimate conversations with her, and call her for prayer. The mantle, which is on her life, is what I desire to gain knowledge of and activate in my life. It was this woman who taught me about the many gateways in my life and the kingdom. In addition, she teaches me how to strategically fight in spiritual warfare. This mother and mentor I love so much is *Tommi Femrite*.

I not only have this mother, but I have several who have tremendous roles in my life, such as *Cheryl Grissom, Charlene Hamilton, Lottie Smith, Judy Buffum-Hemila, Barb Alexander, Sharon Johnson, Gail Gammill, Sheryl Brady* and *Charlotte Moore*. Each of them teaches and guides me in different areas on this journey. Some of them have been assigned to keep my character intact, others have been assigned to teach me sound principles, and some are assigned as prayer warriors in my life. This does not take away from my home church or my pastor, since it is at my home church where I receive the fellowship and corporate anointing. However, the teachings of each mother are tailored made to help me spiritually and naturally. There's nothing like a good home cooked meal made from all natural healthy ingredients served with love from your mom. It is the same with spiritual mothers. They fill you up with the very nutrients you need to keep you growing strong and healthy spiritually.

I wanted to learn about the next level in ministry and in deliverance. Some of the loneliness I felt was because of the transitional phases God was taking me through. I had to learn from the people who were skilled and have already been through the transitions.

As a leader, I needed to glean from other leaders, and as an evangelist I had to learn from other evangelists. If I desired to grow more in wisdom and grace, as well as progress to the next dimension in ministry, then I had to be with and around the very people who were already there.

Women should seek out a mentor who has already been where you are going, knows your personal and spiritual needs, and truly desires you to succeed. Sit at their feet and learn from them. Accept the correction as well as the love, and get as much understanding as you can. The devices of the enemy are wicked and perverse. Find a warrior who has the skills to educate you on warfare, leadership as well as godly character.

Every leader needs someone to talk to who will not judge but help them. Please do not confuse mentoring with friendship. Friendship involves becoming common and familiar. This alone makes it very hard to accept discipline and correction. Mentoring is in a class all by itself. Being mentored involves a different type of serving, obedience, listening and reverence. Though friendship has a known resemblance to mentoring, it involves a completely different mindset. Because of this, many friends will fall away. I have observed when you are being mentored and there is a distinct change which occurs in your life, there are not many who wish to follow and crucify the flesh. It is too much work for a Christian who is comfortable in a dormant place spiritually. Not everyone can make this journey with you and one must be careful about what is more important, a friendship with an individual or a relationship with God.

I had to weigh the cost before I began the course of being mentored. How much did I desire to fulfill the purpose in my life and how much would I forgo in doing so? Was I ready to crucify my flesh and surrender my ways of thinking? Could another individual truly correct me without me having an attitude? How much will it hurt to let go of people, places and things? These are the questions I asked myself before calling *Tommi Femrite* and surrendering my way of knowing and doing things. I chose wisely because I have learned so much about gateways, prayer, intercession and warfare from her. Which brings me to the point of choosing wisely. Be mindful of the qualifications of a spiritual mother for it is a lot like a natural mother. Natural mothers sacrifice and serve as well as teach, educate and love beyond themselves. Make sure your candidate for a spiritual mother has the same and more qualifications. I had a friend who believed she found her spiritual mother but the relationship was more about the suppose mother taking from my friend. You will know if the person is your spiritual mother by the leading of the Holy Spirit. For me, it was as if I found a fresh spring of water when I was at my most thirsty time.

These women came into my life when I was seeking out truth. I needed keys to unlock the doors which were said to be mine. First, I had to find out where are the keys and how do I get them. I also had to be educated on which key unlocked which door and the purpose of the keys. These are things I personally could not learn in church or from friends. I required a one-on-one with someone who could show me, teach me, love me, correct me, protect me and guide me to the next dimension in my ministry and spiritual walk.

Having these mothers as an intimate part of me has been a life changing experience. So much more has been accomplished through their knowledge. The enemy has lost great influence because of the wisdom and understanding I have obtained by gleaning in my mentors' fields.

The Power of Spiritual Sisters

There are other avenues of mentoring which have been a lifesaver to me, my spiritual sisters. Spiritual sisters are people who are prayed up and educated on the devices of the enemy. They encourage you, pray for you and listen to the deepest crevasses of your heart. They always go to the Word of God for answers with you and provide spiritual guidance that puts you right back on track. They walk in the same anointing as you do therefore they understand what you are going through. These sisters for me are *Pam Thum, Renee' Welsch, Azizah Suliman, Sian*

Johnson, Deanna Gammill and my blood sister *Mary Tiller Woods*. They hold me accountable and help me strive towards the mark of the high call.

I strongly recommend all women having spiritual sisters who can be reached at any time to pray you through. Spiritual sisters are an important ingredient to having balance in your ministry and spiritual empowerment.

Having mentors in my life who have invested their anointing and time in me expands the boundaries of the call that is on my life. This in turn helps regulate and administrate the areas of my walk, which needs developing. This takes away the pressure of doing things within my own will and points me to the heart of God.

Restoration Through Spiritual Fathers

One of the ways in which God restored me was through the leadership and guidance of spiritual fathers. I am blessed to have three spiritual fathers, *Howard Tillman, Dana Gammill* and *Herschel Gammill*. These three men redeemed my thoughts of fatherhood in general. Because of the stigma and hurt I felt from my own father, these men were and still are healing instruments used by God to help me continue to grow in forgiveness and kindness. I strongly believe in having spiritual fathers, who are Godly, be a guide to help women understand the relationship of father and daughter. Not in the perverted ways of the world, but in the spiritual structure in which God ordained.

In finding your spiritual father, do not be confused by your feelings or by their status in the community. Emotional decisions tend to lead some women to churches where they easily become vulnerable. Many women develop a spiritual awe and natural infatuation towards the man in the pulpit. This positions the pastor in a place higher then God. This is dangerous and distorts and misrepresents the relationship in which God intended for a spiritual father and daughter, thereby creating a place where offenses and emotional attachments occur. Women must be very careful to make sure they are going to church to learn and serve God and not man. This does not mean that you don't honor the office that is held. It simply means to always check the true motives of your heart. There is only one God. Because of this some women must be particularly careful they are not putting the pastor in the position of filling their empty voids, whether emotional or spiritual. This opens the door to scandal and sexual indecencies.

The title of pastor does not automatically make one a father. Seek out the fruit of the harvest. Look at their ability to reproduce other children who will eventually carry their name. A true father will always guide and love in a spiritual manner. He will consider his daughter as God does, precious and as a queen. Because of this, a godly father will have the spiritual and natural strength and ability to fight on the behalf of his daughter. He is able to discern when something is amiss in her life. He can escort his daughter to the throne room and provide a covering for her. Just as a natural father, he is able to protect and provide for his daughter as well as discipline and direct her. A godly father will cultivate and empower his daughters to become a woman after God's own heart.

Firmly Planted

Jeffery and I have both enjoyed the fruits of our mentors. Being replanted in a place that offered growth and fresh soil was also a key element to our harvest. We were obedient to the will of God by returning to *Cathedral of Life Ministries*. This connection with our church is the foundation for our spiritual growth. Partnering and having the support of your church will build a strong corporate anointing upon you and your ministry. It is a covering unlike no other. Jeff and I have benefited from having this covering and support both spiritual and naturally.

The many roads of travel doing ministry made us tired at times and our church is the river which allows us to be refreshed. We have grown tremendously in our relationship with one another and with God. Our pastor encourages and supports the parachurch ministry of *Ladies Night Out, Inc.* and *L.T.A. Productions*.

This permits Jeff and me to move freely through the nation knowing we have a place to call home.

These numerous bricks of wisdom help cultivate a complete underpinning that will not toss when the wind blows or the storms come. Instead they become a shield that protects you. With wisdom comes knowledge and understanding. Knowledge activates the understanding, such as having and utilizing the benefit of forgiveness, testing and building of one's character, and being mentored as well as being in right partnership. All these combined stimulates growth and provides privileged circumstances. Privileged circumstances are divine opportunities to be a blessing by introducing and leading individuals to the Blesser, for the fear of the Lord, is the beginning of wisdom.

The fear of the LORD is the beginning of wisdom and the knowledge of the Holy is understanding (Proverbs 9:10).

Epoch 4

Lynnette Tiller Appling

A Kept Woman

Established

But now hath he obtained a more excellent ministry, by how much also he is the mediator of a better covenant, which was established upon better promises.
Hebrews 8:6

In the mouth of two or three witnesses shall every word be established.
2Corithians 13:1

Lynnette Tiller Appling

The Promise

Earlier in the book, I presented a brief insight into the promise God has for women. In order to fully grasp what the covenant is between God and women, I must expand on this particular principle in detail. This understanding will help establish your relationship with God and activate the keys to your inheritance. I pray that your mind will be opened and your heart be prepared for the revelation which is needed to slingshot you onto your divine course.

To truly understand the *Covenant, we first must know what a covenant is. A *covenant, which was originated from the word covenire, means to agree.* There are several meanings for this word. It is a *formal, solemn and binding agreement.* It could be *a written agreement or promise.* It could be a *under seal between two or more parties for the performance of some action.* It even means *the common law action to recover damages for breach of such a contract.* All of these levels of meanings are what we will be covering in this section.

In a covenant there must be a *Covenantee who is *a person to whom a promise in the form of a covenant is made.* There also must be a *Covenanter, which *is one who makes a covenant.* A *Covenantor is the party or group of people bound by the covenant.* And we can't forget the *Coventry, who are *the people who are excluded due to lack of knowledge or non-covering of the covenant.* And last but not least, the *Covering, which means *to guard from attack.* Every *covenantor, covenantee,* and *covenanter* must have this.

Right now, we will be re-examining who we are as women in the Lord. I wish to present to you a message of restoration, of promise and of understanding. We will begin with the truth, discover the lie, realize the promise and complete with the revelation of what God gave to us a long time ago.

Then God said, Let Us make man in Our image, according to Our likeness; let them have dominion over the fish of the sea, over the birds of the air, and over the cattle, over all the earth and over every creeping thing that creeps on the earth. So God created man in His own image; in the image of God He created him; male and female He created them. Then God blessed them (Genesis 1:26-28).

Let's take a moment here to look at the word *b*lessed*. This word is derived from the Old English meaning of *blood*. This word *blessed* is equivalent and referred to as the word *anointed. *Blessed* means to *consecrate by religious rite or word* and *anoint* means to *choose by or to designate as by divine election.*

And they were both naked the man and his wife, and were not ashamed (Genesis 2:25).

*Naked here means "*open, visible, not covered by issues, hang-ups, religious boundaries, transparent, totally and completely submitted to God's will.* Not *ashamed means *not scared, not feeling as though they were not covered, complete trust in God.*

*Now the **serpent** was more **cunning** than any beast of the field, which the Lord God has made. And he said to the woman, "Has God indeed said, you shall not eat of every tree of the garden"' And the women said to the serpent, "We may eat the fruit of the trees of the garden; but of the fruit of the tree which is in the midst of the garden, God has said, you shall not eat it, nor shall you touch it lest you die". Then the serpent said to the woman, "You will not surely die for God knows in the day you eat of it your eyes will be opened, and you will be like God, knowing good and evil"(Genesis 3:1-16).*

The serpent represents any circumstance or way of doing, thinking or being that leads us away from the will of God. The serpent has been stated as being the most cunning, which tells me my circumstances, way of doing things, thinking or being will always try to deceive me.

The serpent approached Eve and asked her to tell him what he already knew. I found this part to be particularly interesting. As stated before in the natural, serpents raise their head in order to strike at their prey. With this thought I can imagine Satan rising up to talk to Eve. This means to us as women today that any circumstance, mindset, or stronghold, which raises up already views us of having authority over it, for it must come to eye level (gateway or entrance way to our mind) to tempt and deceive us.

Satan takes the truth, distorts it and perverts it so it becomes seductive to our flesh. In other words, he takes what our spirit craves or desires to be like Christ, twists it and feeds our flesh instead. Now this twist becomes the lie. As women, we are open to it because of our lack of knowledge of who we are and the God-given authority we have.

*So when the woman **saw** that the tree was good for food, that it was **pleasant** to the eyes, and a tree **desirable** to make one wise, she took of its fruit and ate. She also gave to her husband with her, and he ate (Genesis 3:6 BET).*

God created women as emotional beings. However, we tend to serve our emotions, instead of our emotions serving us. We have been blessed with wonderful gifts of being nurturers, administrators, and due to our emotions, people of intervention. At times our emotions can be our strengths. But without godly wisdom they become the ultimate weapon of destruction used to confuse us as to who we should be and who we can be. Satan knew exactly where to attack Eve in order to destroy her and her husband. Her mind became the battleground where he deceived her. The Bible says when *she saw,* and *it was desirable*, she made a decision to following her feelings. How many times have we saw and thought, desired and trusted only to find out these responses were wrong?

However, in this verse we must look at the whole picture. Eve was to be taught by Adam. In truth she knew what was told to Adam since she repeated it, not correctly, back to the serpent. Nevertheless it did not become part of her lifestyle. In other words she did not allow what was told to her to become embedded in her heart.

The fact that her husband Adam did eat so quickly, allows me to know he also, even as close as he was with God, did not understand the cost of this disobedient act. This lack of understanding did not permit him to execute his God given authority to rebuke the serpent and cause restoration to his wife. Instead he chose to yield to his flesh.

If Adam had taken the Word of God and held it close to his heart and passed this along to his wife in a way, which equipped her properly, they both would have successfully defeated Satan in his deception. If they stood on the mandate where God said in Genesis 1:26 that *they would have dominion together over every beast of the field*, and *they were made in the image of God*, then they would have understood the power they had to overcome.

*Then the eyes of both of them were opened, and they knew that they were **naked**, and they sewed fig leaves together and made themselves **coverings**. And they heard the sound of the Lord God walking in the garden in the cool of the day, and Adam and his wife **hid themselves** from the presence of the Lord God among the trees of the garden. (Genesis 3:7 BET).*

Remember every covenant must have a covering. We saw in Genesis 2:25 that Adam and Eve were at one time *not ashamed to be naked*. We unveiled what naked meant in that particular verse. However in this verse, it has a totally negative meaning. Here naked means, **lacking conformation or support, not backed by the writer's ownership of the commodity, contract or security*. Simply stated, Adam and Eve no longer felt as though they had a covering. Each one became their own covering. Eve lost faith in the covering of her husband. Adam decided he was no longer worthy of the covering of God. So both took it upon themselves to do their own thing in their own understanding.

When we get in the state of our own understanding we choose to elude the truth. We refuse to go to church and we begin to stay away from the friends who can tell us when we are wrong. We begin to blame everyone else for our mistakes. We refuse to take ownership. We blame the circumstance. We blame each other. And we will blame God because we don't have the initiative of being good stewards over what He blessed us with.

Then the Lord God called to Adam and said to him, **where are you?** *So he said, I heard Your voice in the garden, and I* **was afraid** *because I* **was naked***, and I* **hid myself***. And He said, who told you that you were* **naked***? Have you eaten from the tree of which I commanded you that you should not eat? Then the man said, the woman whom You gave to be with me she gave me of the tree and I ate. And the Lord God said to the woman. What is this you have done? The woman said, the serpent* **deceived** *me and I ate (Genesis 3:9 ASV).*

The Lord called to Adam not because He could not find him, but to ask him, Where are you spiritually? Why didn't you seek Me for redemption? Why couldn't you usher your wife before Me for restoration? Am I not your God? Didn't I tell you that you had dominion over everything in this world? Would I have not given this world to you and not supplied you with everything you needed to overcome every obstacle you may face? Then tell Me why couldn't you come to Me for guidance, for understanding, for clarity, for forgiveness? Tell Me Adam, what makes you think I canceled this contract? That I no longer covered you? That you are no longer anointed? God is asking the same questions to us as women. Who told us all of the negative things we believe? And why do we believe them? He has created us to be so much more than others perception.

Now, after the conversation between God and Adam, Eve began to realize she had been deceived. The decisions she made were wrong. She understood her emotions guided her to a fleshly passion. This was only pleasurable for a moment. Had she truly known the character of God, who He is... that He is true to this Word. He does not lie. He never abandons. He is always available and that He keeps His promises, then she would have known she could speak to the serpent and it had to obey.

Still, God in His infinite wisdom and His everlasting love because He is the ultimate *Covenanter and the true *Covering of both of them, put into motion the guarantee of restoration for not only Adam but Eve also.

*So the Lord God said to the serpent Because you have done this, you are **cursed** more than all cattle and more than every beast of the field; on your belly you shall go and you shall eat dust all the days of your life and I will put **enmity** between you and the woman and between your seed and her seed. Her seed shall bruise your head and you shall bruise his heel. To the woman He said: I will greatly multiply your sorrow and your conception, In pain you shall bring forth children; your desire shall be for you husband and He shall rule over you (Genesis 3:14 ASV).*

God spoke to the circumstance, the deception and the lie. He rebuked it and cursed it to where it had no power. This serpent will never be able to deceive us again. You should be shouting about this right now.

The serpent representing the lie and the circumstance was cursed to be bruised by the seed of the women. Here is the covenant. God let the serpent or circumstance if you will, know that Eve's seed will be victorious. They will always have the power to overcome the lie. Therefore I present to you the revelation. Women were not cursed. God said He would multiply our sorrow *in our childbearing*. In other words if we were giving birth, we would have pain. Never in the scriptures does it say a woman is cursed. Nor does it say the manifestation of that curse is a menstrual. The Bible plainly states *God cursed the serpent and the ground*. For some reason so many people have believed and taught this lie. I strongly believe this lie is another device created by Satan to destroy women and have control over them. Read the Bible for yourself. Knowing the truth prevents deception and equips you. Please understand enmity means extreme hate, revulsion and abhorrence. Don't be fooled. Women are the ultimate enemies of Satan. You must be girded for the battle. *Wherefore take unto you the whole armor of God that you may be able to withstand in the evil day, and having done all, to stand. Stand therefore, having your loins girt about with truth, and having on the breastplate of righteousness; And your feet shod with the preparation of the gospel of peace; Above all, taking the shield of faith, wherewith you shall be able to quench all the fiery darts of the wicked (Ephesians 6: 13-16).* Without knowledge we perish. *My people are destroyed for lack of knowledge (Hosea 4:6).*

The serpent represents everything that chooses to deceive us. We have the God given authority to rebuke it and speak to it. It must obey.

Now, here is where it gets even better. Eve, being the foremother of us all, received redemption for her mistake. Because of this mistake, God guarantee a divine redemption for women. He then keeps this promise to every woman who chooses to follow him. Here is where we have the *Coventry*. You must choose to follow Christ or be excluded from the promise of redemption. He told Eve her seed will bruise the serpent's head.

God kept this same promise to Sarah who was barren and unable to conceive a child. Sarah embarrassed and ashamed sought to handle things in her own way and was led by her emotions. Sarah neglected to understand the covenant God had with her. Even though she experienced the pain of not being able to conceive, God still redeemed her by giving her a child who would establish the nation of Israel (*Genesis 17:15-16)*

From Sarah we see Ruth, who gave up her gods and chose to follow the one true God. Because she chose to be a part of *covenantor*, God kept His promise He made to Eve. Ruth not only was redeemed from the emotional scars of her husband's death, but through Ruth's womb, God restored Naomi's lineage of promise. Naomi felt as though God's hand was against her. Though desolate and tired, worn and weary, God honored the covenant He made with Eve, which is to always be able to have dominion over our circumstances. Ruth was in the family line of Jesus (*Ruth 1-4 and Matthew 1:1-16).*

Then came Esther, being totally alone in this world due to the death of her *coverings* - her mother and father, Esther was raised up and prepared to be favored by a King. Esther was able to discern the time and the urgency of the moment. Through this she came to an understanding of who she was in the kingdom and what Godly power she had. This understanding positioned her to be used by God to deliver a nation (*Esther1-10).*

From Esther we go to Mary the mother of Jesus and Elizabeth the mother of John the Baptist. Mary who was a young woman was chosen to birth the King through her womb. No doubt Mary suffered from rejection and mourned in her spirit at times during the first stage of her pregnancy. You see in those days an unwed mother was usually stoned to death. So you probably can imagine the torment. Or what about Elizabeth who hid her pregnancy (Luke 1:24-25), old and barren, maybe even feeling a sense of shame because she could not conceive. But God looked upon these women, acknowledging Mary through all eternity as the most blessed out of all, and smiled upon both of them. Restoring their dignity and awakening the divine purpose for their existence, God kept the covenant of restoration He made to Eve (*Matthew 1:18-25 and Luke 1:1-80*)

Let's move on to the woman at the well, who was searching for her identity. Not knowing who she was, she surrendered her body and soul to men in order to find her validity. One day at the well, she met a man who gave her a special of drink from His well. Jesus restored her to her rightful place. God remembered His covenant to Eve through this woman (*John 4:4-27*)

Look at the woman with the issue of blood who spent everything she had and then some trying to find healing for her body, her mind and her soul. You see, once there is a chronic illness in the natural realm, there needs to be healing in the spiritual realm. Nothing happens in the natural without being established in the spiritual (Matthew 16:19). All levels of ones being must be healed. God is a God of covenant and abides by His own Word. He is faithful to do His part. Here again we find restoration and complete healing. The source of healing is Christ. The source of the women being restored is Christ (*Luke 8:43-48*).

Later in the same scripture we find a child who has passed away (Luke 8:49 – 56). In the midst of this distress people are weeping over the death of the child. Jesus speaks to her spirit and her soul. *Damsel arise*, He decrees. Arise above the doubts. Arise above the unbelief. Arise above your circumstance that tells you its over. Arise beyond your childhood fear. Arise and be restored to your natural being. Why? It's because of the covenant. He promised Eve this would happen and so it did.

Then we go back to Mary the mother of Jesus at the cross. She again is barren in spirit. Wondering how she is going to survive the death of her child. Why did this have to happen? Can you imagine the pain of her heart, to see her oldest son face death before her eyes? Can you picture the agony, the hopelessness, and the questions? However Christ, in the midst of His pain continues to look upon Eve and the covenant He made. He says to His mother, *Behold woman your son,* and restores her hurting heart with another son. I noticed He did not call her mother. I believe it is because He addressed the very intimate part of her that was hurting- her womb. If any of you have lost a child, you know what I mean by this statement. Your womb, the very place that held the seed aches when the harvest is destroyed. He called her woman for this reason and in reverence of who she was created to be. This blessed womb of Mary birthed the very instrument that destroyed Satan's reign over our lives. Remember, Satan is women's ultimate enemy. To this day, he is still trying to run havoc and confusion on women. I believe when Christ spoke the word *woman* during His time of establishing restoration for mankind, He completed the healing process for every woman. (John 19:26)

Now my question is what is the lie that keeps you from being who you are predestined to be? God has delivered you from circumstances.

The covenant is this- restoration was guaranteed and delivered at the beginning of time. He then came and gave you the power to succeed. Now Christ is asking what is your excuse? You can't blame Adam because Jesus became the second Adam who covers you and restores you. You can't blame the problem because Jesus cursed it and put it beneath you. You can't say it's your emotions because in dying for you, Jesus gave you the strength and Godly wisdom to overcome. So what is your excuse for not knowing who you are?

I challenge you to understand why God made such a covenant. I implore you to research your identity in Him. Know the truth. Realize you have been predestined, called, justified and glorified for His namesake (*Romans 8*).

As women we face challenges and circumstances that may shake our world. But believe without doubting that Christ redeemed us, and gave us the power to be more than a conqueror (*Romans 8:37*). We don't have to live with the lie anymore. The deception has been uncovered.

God blessed and anointed you to be a woman. Do all things to the glory of God whether it is being the best mother businesswomen, entrepreneur, schoolteacher, waitress, hostess, or janitor.

Your Egypt no longer exists. Don't let anyone try to bring you back to a place that is no longer there. There is no dry land for you to cross over to go back to your past. If they try to take you, take them to the cross and let them know...

I have a Covenant, a divine promise with the Covenanter, the one who made the covenant. It is guaranteed for all the Coventors - people bound by the covenant. If you don't like being in the Coventry - excluded from the covenant and un-covered, come to the Conventer who covers and become part of the Covenant- the promise.

Established

Over the past few years of my life I have seen and experienced the pain of being fatherless, both naturally and spiritually. I have reaped the consequences of not knowing who I was and walking out a life of unforgiveness. Precious time and opportunities were lost because of my ignorance and unbelief. There was much confusion and frustration due to others' negligence and my own disobedience. For this reason, my process of healing was a long one.

Writing the story of my life and bringing some of the pebbles to the surface was another example of God's wonderful mercy and love. I was able to face some hidden issues which needed to be discovered and exposed. The hardest truths to face are the ones that deal with you. Looking in the mirror and seeing someone made into a beautiful swan only comes when you first see the truth of whom you are.

I was once a child broken into many different parts, struggling to breathe, bleeding to death from open wounds, begging to live. During the time of adulthood, I was still trying to grasp some form of air, asking mankind for permission to live, permitting them to create me into who they wanted me to be and utilizing their superficial form of oxygen. I was accepting of them because I didn't have the knowledge or the strength to fight. The lack of love and understanding crippled me as it did my father. My grave was ready. I had one foot in and was sitting down to scoot into the coffin that was carefully designed and built by Satan to succumb to my fate.

But God's love penetrated the depths of my already dug grave. He jump started my heart and stopped the bleeding. Like a skilled doctor, He closed the wounds and became my life support. His Word went through my veins and gave me the antibiotics I needed to survive. His speaking to me blew His breath into my spirit and I became a living soul.

My restoration process was not over because I had to learn to walk again. So God placed me in *spiritual therapy*. He strengthened my muscles by activating my faith. So I would never go back to the grave of despair and unrest, He showed me various weapons and taught me how to recognize and fight my enemy. He sent other warriors. As a result, I would not have to fight alone. During the times I get wounded, He applies His healing balm and restores me to a place of rest.

Today I am a woman once broken by life and restored by grace. I am a warrior, fighting for the cause of truth. Skilled through the Holy Spirit, I have been equipped to fight on many levels. My mentors are continuously teaching me new techniques which are deadly to the enemy.

I am called as a General leading and teaching others how to fight the war on lies, deception and felonious circumstances caused by the serpent. My mandate is to help raise up other broken women to a place of reinstatement, empowerment and hope. Called into the office of Apostle, I help establish cells of warriors in different cities to carry on the work of empowering women and bringing them to a place of relationship with Jesus Christ.

I am established in the Kingdom of God and on earth through my seed and my children's seed. My children and my grandchildren will be warriors in the Kingdom of God, fulfilling the prophecies bestowed upon my household. I am *A Kept Woman.*

A Call For The Broken

My prayer for you, who is reading this story, is to come to a place of intimate worship and understanding. You never have to walk this journey alone. I know it is hard to be without the comfort of men. I've been there. But to be in the arms of God far surpasses the mere moments of affection you may have with a man. I wrote this story for you, the very woman who has given up hope and has freely given away her soul. I know you personally. There is so much I didn't write about, such as being raped and left for dead, the numerous close encounters with death by my hand and others, or about the many relationships I had, but I still understand you.

If you are broken or feel you are unworthy, I am a personal witness of God's unshakable love for you. You do not, I repeat, do not have to stay in the condition you are in!

Maybe you are already saved and are experiencing some of the same things I wrote about, this is for you also. God is a rewarder of those who diligently seek Him (Hebrews 11:6). Seek the face of the Lord. He will answer. He will walk with you and guide you even when no one else will.

I went from dying from open wounds to fullness in life, because I sought His face in the midst of my deepest darkest stuff. And guess what? He came and sat in the stuff with me. Jesus became my passion, as I was always His.

I found out that "I" standing and existing alone was defenseless. I was an island with no connection, no protection and no direction. But "I" joined with Christ became unique,

A Kept Woman

matchless, irreplaceable, one of a kind and distinctive. I was bought with a price that no man could pay. This payment of Jesus' life makes me very valuable (I Corinthians 6:20 & I Corinthians 7:23). You are bought with the same price and you are just as valuable.

There's no magical way of accepting Him as your *Life Support*. The same way someone knocks on your door and you let him or her in, is the same way Jesus works. Open your heart today. Let the wounds be healed by the blood of the Lamb, which brings the spiritual covering.

If you are thinking about making a change that will empower you to move forward in the complete knowledge and acceptance of being restored, and you believe this covenant is for you then pray this prayer:

Lord I recognize Your gift of grace. I believe You are Jesus Christ the Son of God sent to die for my sins and rise again to redeem me to my rightful position. Forgive me for not knowing or understanding who I am in You. Forgive my sins and help me to forgive others. I freely give You my mind, my body and my soul and I surrender up my will. I receive Your gift of covenant and of promise and I thank You for your gift of redemption. I accept Your offer of complete forgiveness and eternal life and I thank You for right standing with You, In Jesus' name, amen.

Please don't allow people to dictate what type of woman you are or give them permission to choose whose woman you are, but be set aside and reserved for the epitome of love. Choose to become a woman who is kept by *grace*, established by the *blood of the Lamb*, and an intimate lover of *Jesus Christ. Be A Kept Woman.*

Lynnette Tiller Appling

A Kept Woman

Information

Coming in 2006

Don't miss out on these newest books by **Lynnette Tiller Appling** coming in **"2006"**. Pre Order your autograph copy today!

A Vessel For Honor

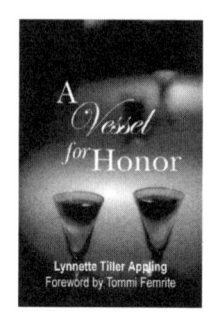

If you have already read **"A Kept Woman"** then this book is the next step in the riveting story of how Lynnette came from brokenness to understanding her place in the Kingdom of God. Gold nuggets illuminate each page as God gently writes His love story to all women in this gripping book.

The Spiritual & Natural Rape Of A Woman

This book takes a deep spiritual and natural look at how Satan uses different strategic weapons to destroy women of all cultures in every area of their lives. Often not talked about in the church is the natural rape of a woman that ultimately creates the elements of spiritual rape. If you've ever experienced rape in either realm then this book is for you.

Forgiving My Mother To Love My Daughters

Lynnette takes you on a healing journey from anger to grief and from hatred to forgiveness. Understanding how to abide in rest through God's identity, she teaches women to break the curses that come from the cycle of insecurity, loneliness, identity theft, illness, abandonment, abuse, self hatred and low self esteem, passed down from mothers to daughters. This book should be read by every mother and daughter.

Lynnette Tiller Appling is the anointed and empowered Visionary & Founder of Ladies Night Out International Ministries, a dynamic women's ministry that has brought tremendous healing and holistic prosperity to spiritually thirsty and hungry women. Ladies Night Out travels the nation and brings international ministries to various cities to help cultivate change and purpose thereby helping the community understand the empowerment principles of the Word of God.

On top of all of this she is as an accomplished National Christian Recording Artist, Counselor, National Conference Speaker, Ordained and Licensed Evangelist and Author of her first book, "A Kept Woman". Her message is one of total and complete healing that truly teaches on redemptive resolutions and empowerment in one's life. Sharing the message of God's promises and often-overlooked covenants He has with women, Lynnette reveals an eye and heart opening look at what Christ has stored up for those who simply believe and obey. Lynnette also teaches and gives consultation on how to prepare ministries in a "Spirit of Excellence" for the next move of God.

She is a yoke-breaking psalmist who understands the power of musical worship, and an evangelist with a clear message of God's faithfulness and undeniable love. Each song and sermon is a direct testimony of what Christ has done in her life. It is unmistakably insightful of how powerful this message is for Lynnette sings and teaches from experience. From surviving rape, poverty, mental & physical abuse, depression, oppression and the death of her oldest child, to being healed from many debilitating illnesses such as fibromyalgia, lumbar disc disease, rheumatoid arthritis, a bleeding ulcer, asthma, ovarian cyst, heart disease & chronic fatigue. These challenges among others have tried to destroy her in the last couple of years. But God has unshackled, healed and released her. He then set her on a course that will cultivate healing, hope, promise and restoration for others.

Lynnette has had the humble honor of opening and ministering for many gospel and contemporary Christian greats such as Tammy Trent, Pam Thum, Anointed, The William Brothers, Vicki Winans, Kenny Eldridge, Jaci Velasquez & Melba Moore as well as a Worshipping Psalmist for Bishop Iona Locke, Pastor Sheryl Brady, Apostle Tommi Femrite, Pastor Cheryl Grissom and Bishop Norman Wagner. Lynnette has also been a frequent requested soloist for the Republican Party's Senator Kirk Schurring. She has had the privilege of being showcased on Total Christian TV, Trinity Broadcast Network, CBS and on local stations in Canton Ohio. Her debut CD "From Within: Psalms of Lament" has been the #1 requested demo CD on Gospeldemo.com for over 40 weeks running in 2001 and is playing on radio stations nationwide. Multiple radio stations have honored her music ministry and she has even been voted as "The Artist of the Year". Her newest CD entitled "Intimate Worship" examines the healing characteristic of God's mercy. This musical rendition of her life is now playing and is available in many stores near you. In addition to the music, Lynnette currently has several speaking DVD's & CD's entitled "A Kept Women", "The Covenant", "Only Believe", "Prepare For the Ark of the Covenant", "Repentance, Forgiveness & Obedience; The Keys to God's Favor", "Purposed Vision" and "Breaking Down the Strongholds" to name a few. Her newest books entitled "A Vessel For Honor" will be released in 2006 along with "The Spiritual and Natural Rape of a Woman" and "Forgiving My Mother To Love My Daughters".

To hear this young lady speak and sing about the stories of her life and the journey from her land of Egypt into the promise land of Canaan, will make you open your heart and your mind to the bold message God brought to her. Lynnette Tiller Appling shares with us a powerful voice delivering an undying message, and a fresh word from God. We ask only that you listen carefully to the message and take hold of what God has to say through this extraordinary woman of God.

Other Products and Teaching Materials by
Lynnette Tiller Appling

From Within: Psalms of Lament Musical CD
Intimate Worship Musical CD
A Kept Woman Teaching DVD
A Kept Woman Video
A Kept Woman Musical CD
The Awesome Love of God Video
The Covenant Teaching CD
Purposed Vision Teaching CD
How To Identify Spiritual Thirst & Famine Teaching DVD
Getting Rid Of The Trash Teaching DVD
Prepare Ye For The Ark Of The Covenant Teaching CD
Forgiveness, Repentance, Obedience; The Key To God's Favor Teaching DVD
Breaking Down The Strongholds Teaching DVD
Only Believe Teaching CD
Victory Over Spiritual Imbalances Teaching CD
The Power of Debt Release Teaching Video by Jeffery Appling

If this book has blessed and empowered you, please send your testimony. We would love to hear from you. Please send all correspondence to:

L.T.A. Productions
4449 18th Street NW, Canton, Ohio 44708
Email: jeffery@LTAProductions.com
Website: http://ltaproductions.com
To have Lynnette Tiller Appling minister at your event by speaking or in concert, please call 1-330-479-9488.

Suggested Reading

These books have helped me in my spiritual walk with the Lord. I believe they will help you also.

Until Love Finds You
The Diva Principle
What Becomes Of The Broken Hearted
Why Do I Say "Yes" When I Need To Say "No"
By Michelle McKinney Hammond

A Woman After God's Own Heart
Beautiful In God's Eyes
Loving God With All Your Mind
Becoming A Woman of Beauty and Strength
By Elizabeth George

Intercessors: Discover Your Prayer Power
By Tommi Femrite, Elizabeth Alves
and Karen Kaufman

Woman Thou Art Loose
By T.D. Jakes

Faith Confessions For The Journey
By Mary Tiller Woods

Intimate Issues
By Loraine Pintus and Linda Dillow

Notes
***All descriptions or meaning of words are from the Scott Foresman Thorndike Barnhart Advanced Dictionary Copyright © 1974 by Scott, Foresman and Company, Glenview Illinois, Used by Permission.

Acknowledgements

I first want to thank my Lord and Savior Jesus Christ for establishing such a seed in my spirit to write to the women who never understood who they are. I thank Him for trusting me to share the story of Our Personal Love Life.

To my husband Jeffery L. Appling, a.k.a. Big Daddy, thank you for being the kind of man who makes everything seem tangible, and provides the necessary tools and guidance to get the impossible to the possible. You are the love of my life, my Boaz. I love you.

To my children Shaila, Joshua, and Garra, you are the beat to my heart. Continue to walk to the beat of God's heart. From my heartbeat to God's heartbeat, this is the way that God ordained it. I love you.

To my mother Paula Tiller, understanding is the first step to healing. When we begin to understand the direction of God's way, He never fails to heal the past and position us for greater favor in the future. Thank you for helping me to understand either knowingly or unknowingly and for being that strong force which keeps me lifted up into His presence. I love you.

To my brothers and sisters Margaret Louise Callendar, James Tarsus Tiller, Mary Tiller Woods, and James William Tiller, this book is for us all. I love you and though we may not know or understand everything about the others experiences, we still share and undeniable love for one another.

To the Lowe Family, Tiller Family and Appling Family, thank you for being a support to me throughout the years. Some showed love in many levels and filled voids I thought could never be filled.

To my overseer Pastor Dana Gammill, Bishop Herschel Gammill and Cathedral of Life Ministries, you came at a time that launched me even deeper into the call upon my life. Thank you for recognizing the call and affirming it. I am forever grateful for your constant support and wisdom.

To my spiritual mothers: **Tommi Femrite, Sheryl Brady, Cheryl Grissom, Lottie Smith, Judy Buffum, Barb Alexander, Charlotte Moore, Charlene Hamilton, Glenneth Tillman and Sharon Johnson** and My spiritual sisters: **Pam Thum, Renee Welsch, Sian Johnson and Deanna Gammill**, - thank you so much for calling the gift out of me. The guidance you have given me is and always will be tremendous. I will never be able to repay what you have deposited into me, but I will always walk and treasure the path you have mapped out ahead of me. I love every last one of you with all of my heart.

To **Tricia Ferguson Brown, Twyla Saulter, Renee Meeks and Dawn Cobb**, each one of you has a very important place in my life and heart. I will never forget what each of you mean to me. Thank you.

To the **Ladies Night Out Directors, Board of Governors and Subcommittee Members**, thank you for your support and commitment. I have taken a part of each one of you. This allows me to continue to progress in the shaping of who God called me to be.

And to everyone who has been a vital part of my life in each epoch of my life, Thank You! What all of you have given me is priceless. Though you are not named (for it will take up the entire book to name all of you), your contributions rather small, large, good or unfavorable have been the developing and creating process of who I am today. Without the experiences of each one of you, I would not understand the pattern of my life that has been gently weaved out by my savior Jesus Christ. For this I am grateful and count every moment as joy.

A Kept Woman

Your Thoughts & Confessions

Utilize some time to renew your mind. Write down your thoughts and confessions and watch God work in your life. Remember, you are A Kept Woman.

Lynnette Tiller Appling

A Kept Woman

Lynnette Tiller Appling

Special Quotes from

A Kept Woman

To Remember

Page #_____
Quote

_____
_____
_____
_____

Page #_____
Quote

_____
_____
_____
_____

Page #_____
Quote

_____
_____
_____
_____

Page #_____
Quote

_____

Lynnette Tiller Appling

Page #_____

Quote

Page #_____

Quote

Page #_____

Quote

Page #_____

Quote

Page #_____

Quote

A Kept Woman

Page #_____

Quote

Page #_____

Quote

Page #_____

Quote

Page #_____

Quote

Page #_____

Lynnette Tiller Appling

Quote

Page #_____
Quote

Page #_____
Quote

Page #_____
Quote

Page #_____
Quote

Hear What Other People Are Saying About This Incredible, Life-Changing Book.

I was so blessed by the book. As I started reading I was so amazed at how God brought Lynnette through all of the illnesses and different things that she went through. I do believe in the healing Power of Jesus Christ. I was so encouraged to see what the finished product was. Thank you for telling us of the wonders of Christ in your life.

-Karen

The part about Overcoming The Spirit Of Fear –really blessed me. I was able to confront myself and have Jesus show me His face. This enabled me to depend more upon Him and less upon myself. In addition, I felt as though this was my life. I could relate to everything that was said. Every woman who reads this story can see a reflection of themselves. This book will help you understand and discover who you are, what area still needs to be healed and what you can become. Thank God Lynnette was obedient to writing this book. I can't wait for my personalized copy of the next one.

-Deana

It was funny. I couldn't wait to get the book home to read it. Suddenly, I couldn't find my book. Holding it and reading it as if his life depended on it, was my husband. You see, we have been through a lot and I was praying for his healing. He wouldn't let me read it until he was done. As if out of no where, he began to change. It was the little things first. He apologized for not being there for me and my kids. His exact words were..."I don't want to be like Lynnette's father." Now, he's becoming the man God desires him to be. This book really does have an anointing to change lives. It's already impacted mine. Thanks Lynnette for hearing the voice of God and writing every women's story.

-Tonya

When I read this story, I just began to highlight the gold nuggets that were carefully laid out in the book for healing. I called all my girlfriends and even bought and sent them a copy. I watched lives change from reading this book and I have a deeper revelation of God's love for me.

-Lanece

I didn't know how to say thank you. I read the book and cried and cried. Thank you Lord for sending this word to my spirit. It was me in the book. Though it was Lynnette's story, it was me she was writing about.

-Darma

There are times in your Christian walk when you wonder if you are the only one going through. You feel alone and anxious, uncertain of what the future will bring. It's the uncertainty – you may have dug a hole so big this time that even God can't pull you out –which brings the greatest fear. Thank you Lynnette for revealing a very intimate part of your life for all to see. You have shown us how to rest in knowing there's no circumstance or situation too dark or too complicated for our God.

-Dawn

A Kept Woman

Appling Family
Photo Album

A Kept Woman

Lynnette

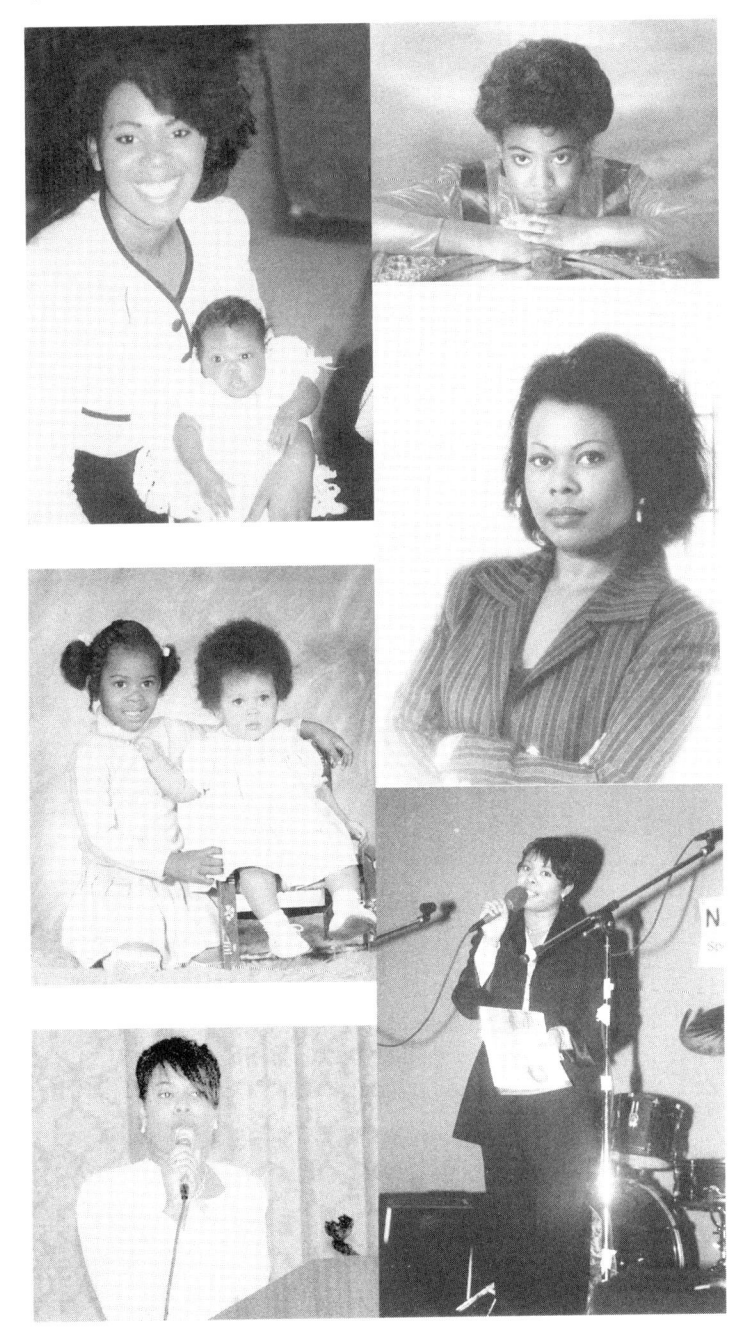

Lynnette Tiller Appling

A Kept Woman

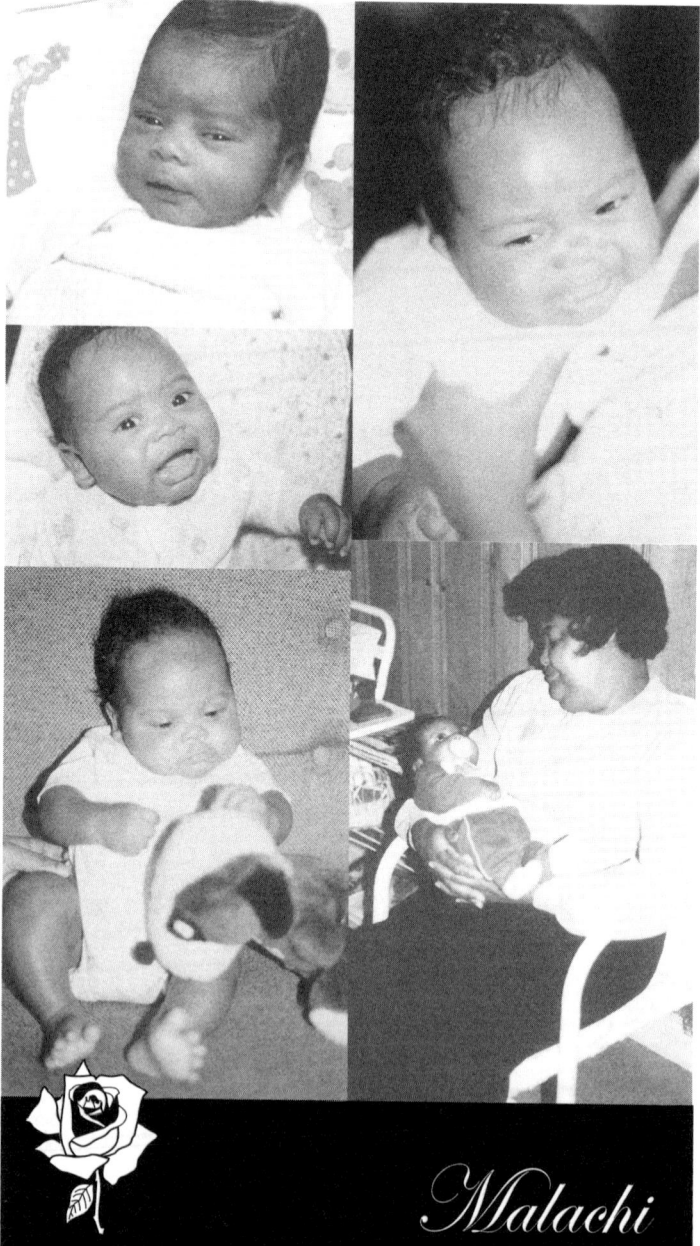

Malachi

Lynnette Tiller Appling

Shaila

A Kept Woman

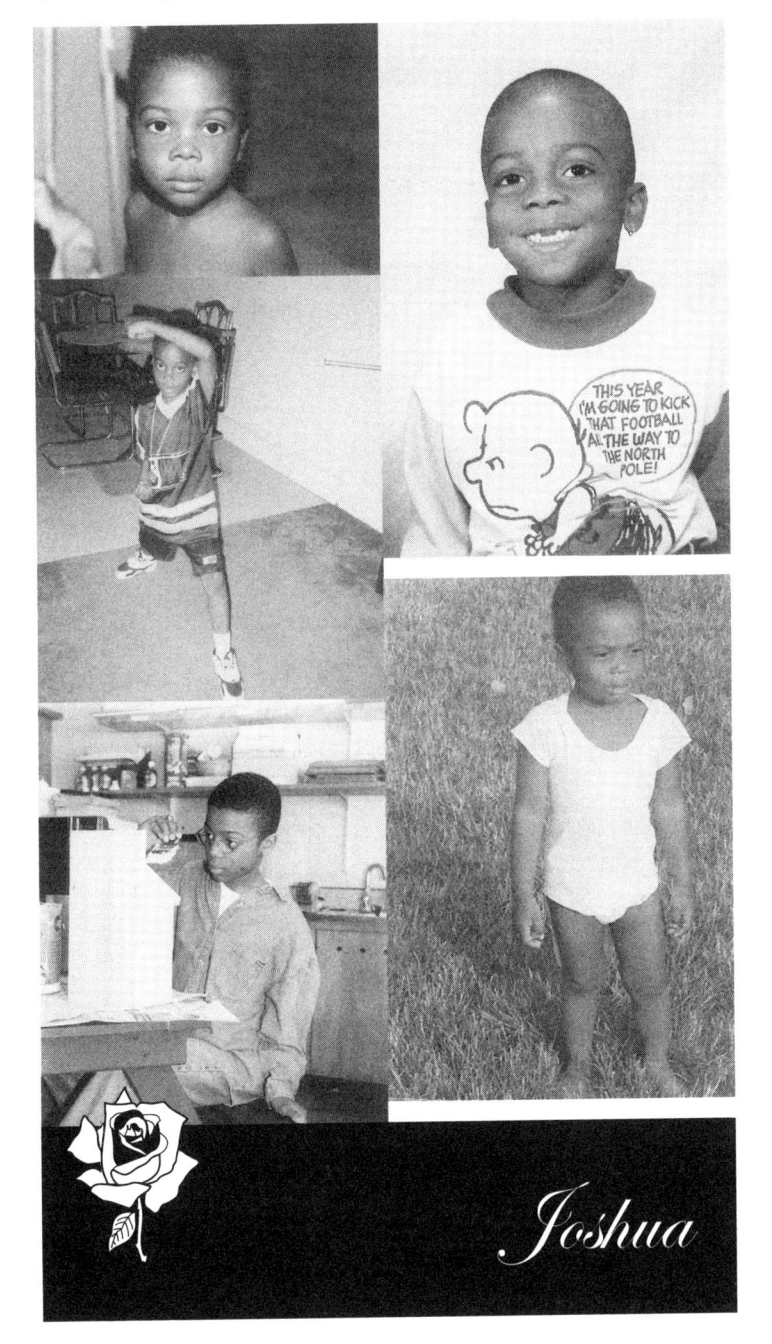

Lynnette Tiller Appling

Joshua

A Kept Woman

Lynnette Tiller Appling

Garra

A Kept Woman

Lynnette Tiller Appling

A Kept Woman

Jeffery

Jeffery & Lynnette